A PROPHETIC CRY

*Stories of Spirituality and Healing
Inspired by L'Arche*

Edited by Tim Kearney

VERITAS

First published 2000 by
Veritas Publications
7/8 Lower Abbey Street
Dublin 1

Copyright © The individual contributors, 2000

ISBN 1 85390 429 5

British Library Cataloguing
in Publication Data.
A catalogue record for
this book is available
from the British Library.

Cover Illustration: 'Walking on Water' by Sally Fitzpatrick.
Reproduced by kind permission of the artist.

Cover design by Bill Bolger
Printed in the Republic of Ireland by Betaprint Ltd, Dublin

*For Maria and Joseph, Stephanie,
Jeremy (safe in God's hands) and Simon*

*I bless you, Father, Lord of heaven and of earth,
for hiding these mysteries from the learned and
the clever and revealing them to little ones.
Yes, Father, for that is what it pleased you to do.
(Mt 11:25-26)*

CONTENTS

ACKNOWLEDGEMENTS

Firstly, I want to thank my wife, Maria, for her constant support and encouragement from the beginning of this project through to its completion. I also want to thank my wonderful children, Joseph, Stephanie and Simon for calling me, at different moments in the editing of this book, out of my head into their world of the heart.

I wish to thank Deirdre Lehane, my administrative assistant, who works in the L'Arche community in Cork. Her great secretarial support as well as her constant good humour and encouragement have been invaluable.

My thanks also to all my brothers and sisters, colleagues and friends in L'Arche for their interest and encouragement and, most especially, for their friendship and support.

I would also like to thank my mother, Ann Kearney, for extending her hospitality to me at *Cuasin*, her lovely home in West Cork, for occasional days of writing and editing. I am also grateful to Mary Hurley, Annette O'Connor and all the staff, along with the Dominican Community in St Dominic's Priory, Ennismore, for their always warm welcome.

I wish to acknowledge the support of Anne O'Sullivan, Hannah Goss, Valerie Ward, Philip Kearney, Sr Stanislaus Kennedy and Richard Kearney. I am grateful for their comments, feedback and advice.

I want to thank the West Cork based artist, my sister, Sally Fitzpatrick for permission to use her beautiful oil painting, 'Walking on Water', on the cover. My thanks also to Mike Foulds for doing such an excellent job in photographing the painting.

It has been a great pleasure for me to work and to collaborate with the editorial and management team of Veritas, and I wish to thank Aideen Quigley, Maura Hyland and Elaine Cox for their professionalism and advice and their enthusiasm for the project.

Lastly, I want to say a special thank you to all the contributors to the book – the authors, the poets and those who gave interviews – for sharing their stories and vision, and for their delight in the gift of language.

Michael Paul Gallagher is an Irish Jesuit, who lectured in English literature at University College, Dublin, for some twenty years before moving to Rome in 1990, where he is now Professor of Fundamental Theology at the Gregorian University. During his Dublin years he taught at least three of the contributors to these pages. Author of several books of spiritual theology, his most regular contact with the wounded of the world has been with ex-addicts.

FOREWORD

The Wisdom of Vulnerability

John Henry Newman, as an Anglican minister, once preached an unusual Christmas sermon, in which he never mentioned the more predictable aspects of the feast. Instead he explored our avoidance of our human 'wounds' as *the* reason why our religious beliefs often remain 'so unreal'. Newman saw this fear of our shadows as the root of all our shallowness. Because 'we dare not trust each other with the secret of our hearts' (this reality of our vulnerability), 'our love is not enlarged' and 'our religion, viewed as a social system, is hollow'. The title Newman gave to his sermon was 'Christian Sympathy', with the implication that if God embraces our woundedness in the birth of Christ, we too are invited into a surprising lowering of our defences.

A Prophetic Cry witnesses to a similar 'upside-down' wisdom, incarnated in the communities of L'Arche. It is a book of personal testimonies rather than of theories. But it echoes that daring insight of Newman: if we let go of shields, we will find new depths and fragilities in ourselves. Vulnerability of that fruitful kind is marked by what Shakespeare called the 'melting mood'. When we let go of mastery, we can enjoy a liberation from surface agendas. We listen differently and with wonder. We admit the uncertainties and agonies behind our facades of control. For many contributors to this book the wisdom of vulnerability came through their contact with people who are handicapped, not just with their pain or limitations but, more surprisingly, with their unique gift of directness and their capacity for love. So these pages are full of counter-cultural paradoxes. Less is more. Walk down the ladder of life, instead of chasing achievement. Let go of your plans to help people: put relationship before knowledge. You cannot change another person: you can only offer presence and slow healing may happen. In the simplest of moments you can be healed of your complexity and recognise the divine.

But these articles are more ambitious than such a quick summary might suggest. They go beyond the psychological to offer stories of slow Christian conversion. When 'helpers' become 'needers', they discover not only hidden layers of sensibility but a whole spirituality of faith. They set the drama of vulnerability within community. They insist that only with the support of others can people face this tough adventure of care. They speak of being severely tested and yet finding the presence of Christ in brokenness. They unite celebration and honesty about pain. They put flesh on the paradox of St Paul that when we are weak, then we are strong.

Although this is not intended as a book of ideas, it manages to touch on some key themes of our so-called post-modern moment. How do we cope with difference? Do we suffer from a lopsided culture, where efficiency ousts deeper relationships? Can our life structures cut us off from the mystery of who we are? Are we imprisoned behind shields of prejudice and of rivalry? Why are we so afraid of crossing boundaries? Is our consciousness of complexity smothering our affectivity? Issues such as these are being pondered in many circles today. But *A Prophetic Cry* offers lived and living answers without getting too absorbed in the questions. In this way it is more than counter-cultural: it suggests where our culture needs healing. Our life rhythms can kidnap us into a double forgetfulness – of the poor, in many disguises, and of our own hearts. We become like those elevators in skyscrapers that are programmed to stop only between the fifth and tenth floors of a building with thirty floors. At the core of this book is the insight that there is a key to opening all the layers of who we are meant to be. That key lies in a spirituality of service, of relationship and of community. To enter into such commitments becomes a gradual schoolroom of the heart and spirit for all involved.

I am reminded of a poem by Adrienne Rich, written in 1962, and entitled 'Prospective Immigrants Please Note'. It evokes the adventure of facing new thresholds of any kind, beyond the prisons of so-called normality. There is a door to go through and then?

> If you do not go through
> it is possible
> to live worthily
>
> to maintain your attitudes
> to hold your position
> to die bravely
>
> but much will blind you
> much will evade you
> at what cost who knows?

Tim Kearney's anthology of testimonies tells us that there is another way of living, beyond the door of individualism and of routine religion. It is both costly and immensely rewarding. In a recent interview Jean Vanier mentions another horizon, not imagined in that fine poem. 'Our freedom starts from the trust that we feel surrounding us'. These pages constitute a hymn to relationships of trust and to their healing power. They insist that this healing is never one-way traffic. The distinction between giver and receiver collapses and a door can be opened towards the Giver beyond and within us all.

Michael Paul Gallagher SJ
Rome, 1 January 2000.

INTRODUCTION

We need to be attentive to the prophetic voices in our lives. There are so many competing voices in our world and even within our own hearts that the prophetic voice can easily get drowned out. Which are the voices that are authentic and that dare to speak the truth and to name reality as it is, even at the risk of disturbing us? Which are the voices that call us to life, to inner healing and to discover more deeply our gift? Which are the voices that point to the presence of God in our lives? They are not always the loudest – or the most articulate or persuasive. They are often the ones we least suspect, the ones that are quite unexpected and surprising.

This book is inspired by the men and women with learning disabilities with whom I have experienced both the gift and the challenge of community life in L'Arche for the best part of twenty years. It tells their story, as well as the stories of those whose lives have been touched by them, mainly through their involvement or encounters with L'Arche.

Many of the contributors to the book speak of their first encounters with L'Arche, when they arrived in readiness to use all their knowledge and expertise to help the members. They found instead a world where the only thing expected of them, indeed demanded of them, was to relate on the level of the heart. Confronted daily by blatant honesty, open-heartedness and trust, they found that many of their defences had no place in this world. They discovered, much to their surprise, bewilderment, amusement and, at times, even delight, that the only thing required of them was to just be. To 'be' together. To be themselves. To be human. This is a place where the heart holds sway and the head, though important and valued, takes second place. The members, many of whom have suffered great hardship in their lives before coming to L'Arche, in the form of prejudice and lack of understanding, have never lost their ability to keep their hearts open. They operate on an intuitive level, with a spontaneity and simplicity that many of us have lost along the way.

In our society, it seems that it is precisely the lack of this ability to relate to each other at the level of the heart that is causing much spiritual strain. There are so many obstacles in the form of appearances, status, knowledge, codes of conduct, that we find it difficult to see beyond these. In L'Arche, the heart is the great leveller, and at that level we are all the same. This can be a humbling and a liberating experience. The contributors explain how this insight has inspired and helped them in their own lives, professions and ministries.

The sense of a prophetic voice and the themes of spirituality and of healing provide the framework for this book. The context is both national and international.

In the national context, this book casts a cool rather than a cold eye on the Ireland of the Celtic Tiger. It does not deny the significant gains and advantages accruing to our dramatically increased prosperity, which is registered in the radical reduction in unemployment and emigration over the past ten years as well as in increased government funding in different areas such as the Arts, the Environment and Health, including services for people with disabilities. These factors have all helped to create a sense of cultural and economic vibrancy in contemporary Ireland, which is something to be welcomed. There is, however, a shadow side to the Celtic Tiger and one aspect of this is that it is undoubtedly leaving a spiritual vacuum in its wake.

A leading Sunday newspaper in Ireland recently commented that the Ireland of the hundred thousand welcomes was fast becoming the Ireland of the hundred thousand millionaires, where traditional thatched Irish cottages were being sold for one hundred thousand pounds and where hundreds and thousands of Irish people were going on annual package holidays to the sun.

Economic progress, however, can cause spiritual strain. Many of the people with disabilities with whom I live and work wouldn't stand a chance in the world of the Celtic Tiger but would quickly be devoured by its competitive and individualistic ethic. In an 'image-driven' consumerist society that markets beauty, physical perfection and wealth, people with learning disabilities do not have a high ranking and are often down at the bottom rung of the ladder. In any event, they themselves are generally more interested in friendship than in finance, more motivated by people than by profit and more inclined to take time to celebrate the gift of friendship than to worship the God of money. In an Ireland that is fast falling into a frenzy of busyness, with people running around in a rush to be successful and make money, without always quite knowing why, people with learning disabilities are quietly reminding us that our health and spiritual well-being lies in attending to weakness not strength, to poverty not wealth.

Like so many prophetic voices, they have a message of non-violence and healing and also a message that challenges our prejudices and preconceived assumptions, and that disturbs us. They call society to change by reminding us that a society, to be truly human, must be founded on welcome and respect for the weak and the downtrodden. They call us, as individuals, to change and to grow by revealing to us that we too are handicapped but that our disabilities are perhaps more subtle and are often more cleverly protected and hidden behind the masks we wear. They reveal to us that personal growth calls us to go beyond our defence mechanisms and the barriers of fear we construct around ourselves and to discover the gift of trust and of human relationships. They also remind us that, in the words of the Charter of L'Arche, 'weakness and vulnerability in a person, far from being an obstacle to union with God, can foster it. It is often through weakness, recognised and accepted, that the liberating love of God is revealed'.

They cry to us and there is a vulnerability in their cry. They need us to walk with them, to support them, to believe in them, and to reveal to them their gift. There is an immense power in their cry, which is a cry for friendship, for recognition and for acceptance. In listening to their cry and in responding to it by becoming their friends and companions on the journey, we discover that, in reality, we need them as much, if not more, than they need us. Just as we call forth the adult in them and help them to assume greater independence, they call forth the child in us and awaken in us the qualities of the heart.

Many people in our modern world are seeking spirituality and healing. This book is also addressed to them and offers them a language and a vision that I hope they will find enabling and empowering and that they can use as a tool with which to dig for the first time, or to deepen, or to begin afresh in their spiritual journey.

The spirituality of L'Arche is based on the revolutionary 'upside-down' vision of the Beatitudes, on the paradox that our spiritual health and healing lies not in the pursuit of power, but in the welcome and integration of weakness, both in ourselves and in the other:

> Blessed are the poor in spirit
> Theirs is the kingdom of heaven.
> Blessed are those who mourn
> For they shall be comforted.
> Blessed are the gentle,
> For they will inherit the earth....
> Blessed are the peace-makers
> For they shall be called sons and daughters of God.
> (Mt 5:1-8)

The gift of this 'upside-down' spirituality is well expressed in the words of Jim Cargin, an assistant who has journeyed in L'Arche for the past twenty years, and who wrote to me recently after a year's sabbatical: 'It is true that each person's life is of infinite value; that there is a mysterious blessing in weakness and poverty, and that God is close to the broken-hearted. I do see L'Arche as a sign of hope, being a means of healing, and a prophetic movement of God's spirit in our times, in our society. As such, it calls attention to the freeing action of God in Jesus, affirming our deepest identity as Beloved, children of a loving Father, who always calls us to true maturity'.

The spirituality of L'Arche is based on a profound respect for the dignity and sacredness of every human person, expressed in the following way in the L'Arche Charter:

Whatever their gifts or their limitations, people are all bound together in a common humanity. Everyone is of unique and sacred value, and everyone has the same dignity and the same rights. The fundamental rights of each person include the rights to life, to care, to a home, to education and to work. Also, since the deepest need of a human being is to love and to be loved, each person has a right to friendship, to communion and to a spiritual life.

As both Jean Vanier and Therese Vanier strongly assert in their interviews, it is a vision of spirituality that is grounded in the human. A vision of the whole human person, where the spiritual and the psychological are not segregated but integrated.

The national context of the book is further re-enforced by the strong presence of Irish voices, be they poetic, philosophical, theological or spiritual in their expression. Some of them are voices from L'Arche in Ireland such as Anne O'Sullivan, Donie Hurley, Danny Canty and myself. Donie Hurley and Danny Canty are both members of the L'Arche community in Cork. In their interviews, they tell the story of their lives from their own perspective as people with learning disabilities. Others are voices from different professions, ministries or organisations in Ireland such as John Gibson (music), Richard Kearney (philosophy), Fr John McCullagh (theology), Fr Brendan Kelly (priesthood), Anne Gibson (Faith and Light), Sr Stanislaus Kennedy (Focus Ireland), Rev Ruth Patterson (Restoration Ministries), Dr Michael Kearney (Hospice). All of them, in their own way, friends and fellow-travellers of L'Arche, who have been touched in some way by its spirituality and vision. The poetic voices are nearly all Irish. Some, such as Anne McKeon, Fr Bernard Allon and Peter Brabazon are people who work in, or are associated with, L'Arche. Sodilva Murphy is the parent of a child with a disability. Others, such as John Montague, Aidan Mathews, Pádraig G. Daly, Pat Ingoldsby and Anne Kelly are established Irish poets in their own right.

The book, however, also has a broader international context. Many of the questions explored go beyond an Irish and national framework: What is the key to living an authentic spirituality in the modern world? What are the core values of Christian spirituality? What are the main challenges facing the Christian Churches, as we enter into a new millennium? The spiritual crisis in Western civilisation and the sense of incipient chaos arising from the widespread breakdown of human relationships, in general, and of community and family life, in particular, is also explored and expressed in different ways in the book, along with the birth of a new vision of spirituality and healing that is truly ecumenical and universal, and that gives grounds for a renewal of hope.

These questions are touched upon in some of the articles and poems in Part One, but they are given particular attention and focus in the interviews in Part Two. It is worth mentioning that my interview with Jean Vanier, *The Power to Make Human*, is in fact an amalgamation of two separate interviews. I conducted the first interview with him as a post-graduate student of Anglo-Irish Literature in UCD in Dublin in 1980 for a special issue of *The Crane Bag* journal, which I was editing, on the theme of minorities in Ireland and Church/State relations. I did the second interview with him more recently in Trosly in France in 1999. It focuses on the themes of spirituality, healing and the prophetic voice of people with learning disabilities.

The international context of the book is also witnessed in the presence of contributors from France (Jean Vanier), the UK (Therese Vanier), and the US (Curt Armstrong). This reflects the international nature of L'Arche as an organisation.

Strong links exist between L'Arche in Ireland and L'Arche in Trosly, France – the L'Arche community founded by Jean Vanier in 1964, where many of our current community leaders and assistants in Ireland lived and worked for a time and were deeply shaped and formed by the experience. I am grateful for this bond of friendship and of support with Trosly as well as that which exists with the communities in the UK, Africa (L'Arche Uganda in particular), the US, Canada and indeed throughout the Federation.

I am also grateful for the presence of Faith and Light in the book through the inspired voices of Anne Gibson, Fr Brendan Kelly and

Curt Armstrong and the mutual friendships and connections that continue to grow here in Ireland between our two organisations, which are two branches of the same spiritual family and which have now grown to include Faith and Sharing (Retreat Movement) and Faith and Friendship (Ministry of Reconciliation). Some of the parallels and connections between L'Arche and the Hospice movement are another interesting feature, particularly in the interviews with Dr Michael Kearney and Dr Therese Vanier.

In conclusion, let me say that this book does not endeavour to idealise L'Arche or people with learning disabilities in any way. It does not deny the reality that disability is painful and that living in L'Arche is often hard. It does, however, give expression to some of the wisdom and inspiration that people with learning disabilities have shared with me, and with many of the other contributors to this book. It bears witness to their power to unwittingly transform hearts and to call forth in us the gift of what it means to be human.

Tim Kearney
January 2000

PART ONE

John McCullagh is a priest of the diocese of Derry. He set up the first SPRED units in Derry city, which catered for the religious development of the handicapped. He has been a frequent broadcaster with BBC radio and television and with RTÉ. The handicapped has been a recurring theme in many of his talks. At present he works with the National Centre for Liturgy and with Kairos Communications, Maynooth.

THE PROPHETIC VOICE
OF THE POOR

For years the face of my country was tragically familiar on the television sets of the world. For all its natural beauty, its lakes of Killarney, its mountains of Mourne or the wild ruggedness of its Atlantic coastline, it was the pain-stained face of the country that was recognised throughout the five continents. Too many of our flags were black and too many of our parades led to the cemetery. Children who in other times would have chased a bouncing ball became experts on weapons of war, and death became, for so many of them, a way of life. Indeed, it was at a child's funeral, another by now forgotten victim of crossfire, that I became aware of a voice calling for peace for the sake of God if not for the country. A Northern Irish poet, John Montague, expressed that funeral in these moving words:

> Unmarked faces
> fierce with grief
>
> a procession of children
> led by a small coffin
>
> the young
> mourning the young.

>A sight beyond tears
>beyond pious belief

>David's brethren
>in the land of Goliath.

After the funeral there was the inevitable riot, and following a baton charge I found him, a small cowering boy crouched in a doorway, looking after a terrified kitten. He heard nothing of the abuse that was hurled with the stones or the sounds of war, for he, the teenage Down's Syndrome boy, had a life to protect, a precious life that he had to preserve because a kitten crossed his path. One of David's brothers was here in this land of Goliath – miles away from the dusty days of the Old Testament.

Jesus, Prophet of Poverty

God has a biblical reputation for stooping down to those who crouch and cower. If God has a weakness, it is for those who are on the margin, without prestige or power – those who seemingly exert no influence over the everyday lives of people or nations. The Greek word St Luke uses for the poor – the *ptochos* – derives from the word meaning to crouch or to cower. These are the people of God who feel they have no claim on God's time or attention, for they stand before him without the trappings of influence. But their very attitude disposes them to turn towards Jesus Christ for salvation and the dignity of his friendship. This same Jesus Christ, throughout the pages of the New Testament, identifies himself time and time again by the community he has formed – the community of the poor.

Indeed, before his birth, his mother in her magnificent prayer saw herself as the personification of the poor. Luke makes her their spokeswoman, the perfection of their poverty. In days of simple lifestyle, Mary prepared for the coming of Christ. Eating the bread and wine of Nazareth, she put flesh and blood on the growing child in her womb. Then she came to Bethlehem, and in the shocking starkness of a shepherd's shelter, she waited for the Messiah as the night winds and the last breaths of Old Testament times were blowing over her. And her son was born. Throughout his life his poverty remained total and fundamental. Unlike a tourist to a developing country, Jesus had no return ticket. This Messiah identified himself completely with humankind. There was even that high point of dependence on others when he needed help to carry his cross. He lay on the wood of a manger, wrapped in swaddling clothes at birth. At his death he was stretched naked on the wood of a cross. Some people made a fuss at his funeral – they buried him with the trappings of the rich.

When we read the New Testament carefully, we discover that it continually adopts the perspective of the poor. E.W. Monnich in his book *De Koning te rijk* puts it strikingly. 'The first Christians', he says, 'looked on life from the perspective of the outcast, the helpless, the prisoners and the condemned.'

In the parable of the good Samaritan, Jesus looks on human life from the gutter. It is through the eyes of the victim that we see the priest and Levite pass by and the Samaritan take time to stop and care. Monnich again suggests that Jesus looks at life from the beggar's point of view because he himself is one of the beggars and he makes the point that faith is more a perspective than a conviction. You and I would rightly feel a sense of revulsion if a Government official visiting a refugee camp comforted the starving homeless with the words 'Blessed are the poor', but when Jesus says the words we remember they come from a Messiah whose solidarity with broken people is more a matter of deeds than words.

Jesus Christ's 'vicarious poverty', as Hans-Rudi Weber calls it, is a deliberate identification with the suffering servant in Deuteronomy-Isaiah, who is so often recalled in the Gospel of Matthew:

> Here is my servant whom I uphold,
> my chosen one in whom my soul delights.
> I have endowed him with my spirit
> that he may bring true justice to the nations.
>
> He does not cry out or shout aloud
> or make his voice heard in the streets.

He does not break the crushed reed,
nor quench the wavering flame.
(Is 42:1-2)

And again in Isaiah 53:

Like a sapling he grew up in front of us,
like a root in arid ground.
Without beauty, without majesty (we saw him),
no looks to attract our eyes;
a thing despised and rejected by men,
a man of sorrows and familiar with sufferings,
a man to make people screen their faces;
he was despised and we took no account of him.

Jesus Christ, with no position, no investments, no political power, had no charity to hand out as agencies do nowadays. People whose hands are empty have nothing to give but themselves, and that was the essence of the life of Christ. You will remember that when he rose in the synagogue at Nazareth, the passage he chose to describe his mission was 'The Spirit of the Lord has been given to me. He has sent me to preach the good news to the poor' (Lk 4:18). It would be a challenging motto for any new bishop!

The Age of the Prophets
We still live in biblical times for God still reveals himself in and through the headlines of each day. The face of the earth is blistered with battle marks and so much of every day's news is the thundering reports of war. From Kosovo to the Sudan, from Ireland to Iraq, people continue to give their minds to peace but their hands to war. There may still be those who feel that war is an inevitable part of human history and that this human bloodsport is a check on the world's bulging population. In recent years we have made the world smaller and, as the instruments of war increase, it must dawn on all of us that there can be no spectators because the arena of war today cannot be guaranteed to stay in the selected zone of battle. We all

know it's too late to have a passionate desire for Christian peace and justice when tanks destroy lawns in peaceful suburbia anywhere in the world. Blood sacrifices are still being offered on altars of conquest, on altars of greed and ambition, on altars of revenge or political expediency. The world, still with its ring of nuclear weapons, is surely the land of Goliath. Is there any place left for the brethren of David?

We may be tempted to think, now and again, that if Jesus Christ took on our flesh and blood and pitched his tent amongst us, perhaps he has now picked up his tent and quietly stolen away.

In every age there have been prophets, men and women whose ears are so finely tuned and whose eyes are so delicately focused that they see the movement of God in the events of days past or in the screaming headlines of today's war-weary world. There were the prophets of the dusty days of pre-Christian Palestine, there have been the Christian men and women who, after lives of service, were canonised, and today people like John Paul II, Teresa of Calcutta and Jean Vanier allow their lives to point to something beyond the smoking horizons of today's emptiness.

Sometimes I think we spend too much time searching out the articulate Christian, or making world-wide pilgrimages in search of gurus who might make sense of our suffering or give purpose to our pain. The prophets of old had the distinction of getting little attention from their own people and little welcome from their local community. Jesus Christ came to his own and his own people did not receive him.

For a number of years now I have heard the words of the prophets in the confused mumbling speech of the mentally handicapped. I have found the presence of God in the gentle presence of these people whose wounded nervous systems and peculiar limbs don't ever merit the headlines of even the local newspaper. The prophets of the Old Testament were all people of action. When God commanded them, they got to work, thundering out their charges against king or priest. But not all prophesying is thundering God's word or threatening his wrath. God can speak in silence. Elijah, one of those old prophets, learned this lesson on the mountain a long time ago:

'Go out and stand on the mountain before the Lord', he was told. 'Then the Lord himself came by. There came a mighty wind so strong it tore the mountains and shattered the rocks before the Lord. But the Lord was not in the wind. After the wind came an earthquake. But the Lord was not in the earthquake. After the earthquake came a fire. But the Lord was not in the fire. And after the fire came the sound of a gentle breeze. (1 Kings 19:10, 11, 13)

Whenever we gather with the handicapped we are in the presence, I think, of many gentle prophets. Sons and daughters called and marked by God for a special mission in life, and because of their handicap they speak to us every day in the quietness of their lives, if only we would listen. It is true that those in our community who suffer handicaps of the mind and nervous system need the support and encouragement of the local Church, but it's more important, I'm beginning to think, to realise that the Church, in our time, needs the witness and prophecy of the mentally handicapped. We live in an age when our worth is largely measured by possessions, when even the joy we have seems to be got on credit. We worry about tomorrow, about the growing hazards to health, about pain and parting. We are wrapped up in ourselves because we feel unable to cope with anything else, and the handicapped quietly ask us: where is all the knowledge we are losing in information? where is the wisdom for all our knowledge? where is the life we are losing in our lifestyles? They try to tell us about the emptiness of great possessions in a world where we are refugees, running from one crisis to the next. They challenge our anxiety with the peace of mind and sense of security they have found in the goodness of those who continually care for them. They tell us something else. They underline the value of each human life.

Do you remember the outcry in the Gospel story when Mary, the sinner, knelt at the feet of Jesus and anointed them with expensive ointment. 'Why all this waste?' was the chief concern of those who were never guilty of an act of such extravagant kindness. There are those today who look into the pram of a handicapped child and ask the same question. 'Why all this waste?' God, however, makes no mistakes.

If he gives a child a restricted life, he may be asking the rest of us, whose handicaps are not so obvious, to begin to realise that we are not measured in his eyes by intelligence tests, feats of endurance, or outstanding skills. In a world where we are slow to trust each other, these handicapped children of God reach out to every one of us as a friend and trust their neighbour with little hesitation. In a world where we measure ourselves against the progress of our neighbour, they treat us as equal. In a world where we are jealous of the achievements of others and where heads are crowded with thoughts of envy, they have no room in their minds for trivialities of that sort. In a country where denomination marks us as different, they have no use for labels that divide. They don't plan for peace because they offer threats to no one. They take life a day at a time, people one at a time, friendship, an embrace at a time. They don't talk love. They live it. These are the gentle prophets in an age of comfortless sounds.

So it is today that the Messiah, a master of disguise, comes among us under the appearance of these hidden prophets and, in a world where the media and communications underline achievement, he speaks to the world, not in the highly articulate phrases of the trained communicator, but in the halting language of these poor.

A Sign of Contradiction

The old prophet Simeon met the mother of Christ in the temple and, on taking her child into his arms, he described him as a 'sign of contradiction'. Such a worthy title could be given to every handicapped child at baptism. For here is a person whose presence is a continual challenge to you and me, who feel that we might be able to get joy on credit for a few days with a banker's card or an hour of fleeting recognition. Here is a child of trust in a world where the word has largely lost its meaning. Here is a child of love who reaches out to all. Here is a child of faith who accepts every stranger as a friend. Here is a child of peace who is a source of joy in a valley of tears. Here is the innocent who won't hurt or destroy but whose life can touch the depth of ours and call forth any sources of goodness and compassion that lie hidden there. Here truly is a sign of contradiction.

Other Hidden Lives

The history of the mentally handicapped in any society has not been so much *their* history as the history of what others have done or not done for them. Jesus was so sensitive to people that he never treated them as objects of study or pity. Mentally handicapped people are still as hidden from history as they are from the rest of life. In the Irish language there is no word for mental handicap – they were simply known as *daoine le Dia* – the people wrapped up in God. While the sentiment was lofty, the care we offered to them as a Church was tantamount to sinful neglect. We went on to measure them in terms of the head more than the heart, and Canon Law confined them to their pews at Mass but did not allow them to sit at the table of Christ for the Eucharist. The sight of a Down's Syndrome altar boy or a brain-damaged girl on the altar would have been a case for parish discussion. No, even the Church underlined their difference and made them marginal people – people with hidden lives.

Jesus Christ, the prophet of the poor, the marginal, the bypassed and the forgotten, had his hidden life for all the years of Nazareth. Yet in all those years of his boyhood and manhood the land of Judaea and Samaria was full of people pontificating about their version of God, while Jesus the saviour was amongst them, unknown, undiscovered and, in their eyes, unimportant.

One Suffering Servant

My native parish, on one occasion, had an idea of inviting back all its sons and daughters who had made some significant contribution to the whole nation. There was one man who was respected for his political contribution, another for his writings in Irish, and yet another for his work in education. Inevitably there would be a few priests and nuns who had brought the news of the gospel to far-flung mission fields, and a Christian brother who worked in India. As I got to thinking about the list, I came to realise that the man who had made the biggest contribution to me was Joe, the delicate Down's Syndrome boy who had been the companion of my childhood days. He didn't make the platform with the parish notables but I told his story to a world audience on a BBC world service programme. I think it underlines all I have said so far.

It was in the smoke-filled room of a little country pub, which gloried in the title of 'Hotel', that I found myself one winter evening for the birthday party of this remarkable man. Despite the cautious words of the family doctor at his birth, he had lived to see his thirtieth year, and his friends, who were many, had decided to express their admiration and gratitude to him in a way that didn't call for words. I first knew him as a delicate Down's Syndrome boy who hadn't the breath for games or the heart for leaving his mother to mix with the neighbours' children. Now here he was, sporting a new suit, and exploring the intricacies of the new transistor the local lads had bought him.

Everybody knew him, and everyone in ten townlands, at least, realised that, despite his obvious handicap, he had brought a certain gentleness to our lives and had forced all of us to look at ourselves a little closer. Here in this country where geography had made people neighbours, and history tried to make them enemies, he saw no borders. He believed in people, he worried with the families of the sick, he wept at our funerals and was saddened by the life's blood of the Sperrins draining away in emigration. His country to him was more about people and living than about territory and dying. When he prayed, he didn't rely on words. He was Catholic, Presbyterian, Anglican, Methodist and Baptist, since there was no room in his mind for the details of doctrinal division, and when the Salvation Army or the Brethren expressed their praise in song on Saturday evenings in the town, he would, with obvious delight, give rhythmic support to God.

His politics were simple too. Every man and every woman and every child was his country, and flags were only for flying at festivals. He wore a shamrock on St Patrick's Day with the same enthusiasm as he sported the orange emblem in July, and, at election time, he travelled the country with whichever friend gave him a lift.

The age of the prophets, we sometimes think, were those dim distant years long before Christ tramped the dusty roads of Palestine. Isn't it strange how seldom it strikes us that God still chooses the weak to confound the strong in times when the strong do little more than confuse the weak. The birthday party was the honouring of such a prophet who spoke a simple message of love and life in the face of news bulletins about hate and death. He whispered hope against ghettoes who screamed out their denomination; and when he was misunderstood or hurt by the callous remarks of those who didn't wear their handicaps so openly, he didn't ration out his measured forgiveness. He smiled and walked away. On the night of his birthday, at least, he wasn't without honour among his own people.

The local bakery delivered a cake towards the end of the night. It had no candles, but then, I thought, it didn't need any. When one man lived out Christ's invitation to be a light in the world so perfectly, candles lost their symbolism and meaning. Someone turned on his transistor for a football result before we left. News headlines told of heartbreak in another two homes. He picked up his present and faced the outside darkness with a smile. The prophet had yet a long way to go.

The world stands in need of a prophetic voice. Too many wait to weigh the words of religious leaders before making any commitment. Perhaps the voice of Christ is calling out again to his own people but we are listening on predictable frequencies. The real presence of Christ under the appearance of the flesh and blood of the least of our brothers is challenging us to live out our faith, but we spend so many hours seeking the living among the dead, like Magdalene on the first Easter morning. The Christ who was one with the poor of Israel all those years ago is one with the poor of a third world within the boundaries of all our countries. Someone once suggested to me that perhaps the handicapped hear sounds we don't hear, see other colours, live in a world in which we can have no part.

You and I may need to empty our minds of the frivolity that we call seriousness, open our eyes to wider visions, and open our hearts to a love that leaves self at home. Maybe if we kept a green bough in our hearts, the singing bird would come.

When life ends for the many who have known the privilege of being a fellow pilgrim with the handicapped and when those who become poor in order to share their path finally come to Christ, I'm sure he will welcome them home with familiar words, 'Come blessed of my father, I was a stranger and you brought me in. I, the Christ of the poor, walked the earth with you in that carefree little child with the soft sad eyes'.

CHROMOS

Reluctantly you journey to the outer world
Too frail for the rigours of labour
Your ailing, feeble body falters
Inching its way in breech position.
Birth comes with deafening silence.
Your sloe-like pallor confirms
months of agony, suspicion, fear;
Shifting, darting, oblique glances imprison me
Inwardly screaming, begging to be told.
No-one hears.
No-one wants to hear.
'It's a boy,' they say with feigned assurance.
'Is he Down's?' I ask.
No-one answers.

Your imperfections turn my mundane, tranquil existence
Into a frenzy of silent screaming,
Blind panic, trapped in a windowless, doorless dungeon.
Despair.
Deep grief envelopes me.
'A child of God, a saint for a son', they chorus.
Pious platitudes reverberate around me.
Why does he have to be?
He is not the child I carried,
This alien they foist upon me.
My life freezes.
No future.
No hopes.
No horizons.

Yet He who ordained this trial
Was to graciously support me.

Your winters count to six now.
Unwittingly these years uncover
The mettle from which I'm made.
Your being is the kingpin of our home;
In us you have tapped that which
lay dormant before your coming.

Together we have climbed the peaks,
Endured the troughs,
Cavorting with death, yet running away again,
Growing stronger, ever happy.
Loving unconditionally.

Today we strolled together in the glen,
You pulled your hand from mine
To greet an abandoned, homeless man by the river.
You hugged him with all the power
of your precious being.
His moist, sad eyes looked up at mine.
'Nobody ever kissed me before,' he slurred.
Six winters ago they told me you would die;
That you were handicapped.
Today you touched and loved the unwanted.
If you are handicapped
What then, are we?

Sodilva C. Murphy

Richard Kearney studied at University College, Dublin, Magill University, Quebec, and La Sorbonne, Paris, where he was a student of Paul Ricoeur. He is currently Professor of Philosophy at UCD and Boston College. He is married to Anne Bernard, and has two daughters, Simone and Sarah. He is author of several books on contemporary thought, culture and politics, as well as two novels and a collection of poems. His publications include Poetics of Modernity, The Wake of Imagination and Postnationalist Ireland.

COME AND HAVE BREAKFAST

For Alexandre and Isabelle

My father called them *l'archites*. It had a biblical ring to it. Like Cushites, Canaanites, Hitites, Amorites. One of those wandering tribes of ancient Judaea or Samaria. But it had another kind of ring too that had nothing to do with the Holy Land.

'The l'archites are coming', my father announced one Easter Saturday, standing at the front window of the family house in West Cork, a set expression on his face. He was referring to a vanful of jubilant beings arriving from the L'Arche community in Cork, of which my brother Tim was the director. They were arriving, with Tim at the wheel, to spend Easter by the sea.

With the active collusion of my mother, and in spite of my father's grumblings, the l'archites took over the entire house for three days, invaded the living room, monopolised the sofa, devoured the food (before, during and after meals), fiddled with the TV and video controls, and embraced my father with great bear-hugs whenever the spirit moved them.

The word l'archite had a nice ambiguity about it. On the one hand, it meant quite simply someone who came from L'Arche, a community for handicapped persons first founded by Jean Vanier in the village of Trosly-Breuil in France. It was French for the Ark: a place or refuge for the wounded, fragile and discarded. On the other hand, it carried a double meaning for someone like my father, who was convinced that while the handicapped visitors were indeed heaven-sent they were also obstreperous invaders! In that mischievous Franco-Irish expression – l'archite – the eschatological and the scatological went hand in glove.

Humour was the operative mood. After the initial shock of their arrival, the handicapped gradually succeeded in cheering up my father. Once he accepted that his house was no longer his own for the duration of their visit, he began to relax and enjoy the occupation. By the end of the second day he was actually sitting and talking with the l'archites about everything from rugby matches and the weather to the latest international news. In fact, he talked far more with them than he ever did with any of us, his seven children. He was particularly amused by their original turn of phrase and uninhibited expression. Discretion and decorum flew out the window as unbridled affection rushed in the door.

Over the year my father became especially friendly with two members of L'Arche: Donie Hurley from Tim's community in Wilton in Cork and Jacques Bregola from the L'Arche community in Trosly-Breuil, which my brother Philip, a priest, was then serving. Jacques (a true Gallic patriot) was partial to rugby. He could never accept anything less than a total French triumph! Indeed, that particular Easter Sunday when Ireland were leading France by ten points in Lansdowne Road with just five minutes to go, Jacques announced that the Irish team were in blue and the French in green. He cheered the green to victory! *Allez les verts!* My father considered the ploy quite ingenious and enjoyed Jacques' resourcefulness even more that the Irish victory.

He appreciated Donie's resourcefulness too. Especially that Easter Sunday morning when he answered a knock on his bedroom at four a.m. to find Donie standing there with a tray full of chocolate eggs. 'Breakfast is ready!' Donie proudly announced to my bleary-eyed parents.

When my father died in 1996 two of the most grief-stricken mourners were his L'Arche buddies. Donie insisted on walking up to the altar in the church in Cork city and contributing to the funeral oration by publicly declaring 'I loved that man'. Jacques made the journey from France to be present for the occasion and to pay his respects.

In the early days my family was somewhat divided between those who had a special commitment to the L'Arche community – initially associated with the Faith and Light group in Cork – and those who had not. The first wing, comprising my three brothers, Tim, Philip, and Michael, along with my mother and sister Sally, and sister-in-law Marian, had a special rapport with Jean Vanier, whom they had met and befriended in the late seventies. My three brothers and sisters-in-law would spend long periods working with the handicapped in Vanier's own community in Trosly-Breuil, and two of them still work full-time for L'Arche communities. By contrast, the other wing of the family, led by my father, and including myself and my younger brothers, John and Peter, were less enthusiastic (if by no means hostile). At first, it is true, we slightly resented the open-house policy towards the L'Arche community while sharing a deep admiration for Vanier and his pioneering vision. But over time, as we observed our father's mellowing attitude towards his L'Arche pals, our initial resistance melted. Like my father, I too gradually warmed to the L'Arche vision.

It is difficult to explain how and why. Apart from the anecdotal encounters with individual handicapped persons, like those above, or with Vanier himself (an inspiring presence), it is hard to convey how the spirit and humour of L'Arche can touch one. So rather than reminisce further here about encounters of the first kind, I will try to communicate how my understanding of L'Arche helped me better appreciate some of the most basic messages of the Gospel. I refer in particular to the suggestion that the kingdom of heaven is a mustard seed. In other words, that it is in the little that the great manifests itself, in powerlessness that strength resides. Or to put it in a somewhat more contemporary idiom: that less is more.

As I was trying to summon up some ideas for this article, I happened to be visiting Israel with my wife, Anne, and my two daughters, Simone and Sarah. On 4 April 1999, we arrived in Tel Aviv early enough to make Easter Sunday Mass at the small French

Benedictine monastery of Abu Ghosh, the alleged site of Emmaus, located some eleven miles west of Jerusalem. During the simple uncrowded ceremony, accompanied by plain chant, I could not help being struck by the Gospel reading: Jesus appearing to his disciples on the road to Emmaus (Lk 24:13-35). The first thing that hit me was how two disciples walking on the road failed to recognise their Messiah when he appeared. In a wonderful twist of irony, Jesus asks them what they are talking about: to which they reply that he must be about the only person in Jerusalem who hasn't yet heard about Jesus being crucified!

Continuing the game, Jesus asks the disciples to tell him all. They do, even mentioning – with doubled irony – how the apostles who went to the empty tomb on hearing that Jesus had risen 'did not see him'. Jesus scolds them gently for not believing what the prophets had taught, thus making it necessary for the Messiah to suffer crucifixion before entering into his glory. But still they do not see him. Only, finally, when Jesus agrees to stop off at the village of Emmaus and share their evening meal, are the scales lifted from their eyes. In the breaking of the bread they at last recognise him. As soon as they do, however, as soon as their 'eyes are opened', Jesus 'vanishes from their sight'. No sooner does he appear than he disappears. Now they see him, now they don't.

Several things about this story remind me of the 'prophetic cry' of L'Arche. We do not recognise the sons and daughters of God there where they appear to us as we wander along the road of life. So full of great expectations are we that we fail to see the divine in the simplest of beings. Second, God cares for our physical and material being: it is in the sharing of food that he makes himself visible. And third, rather than glorying in some kind of I-told-you-so posthumous triumph, Jesus takes his leave. As soon as he is seen, he absolves himself, goes invisible, refuses to be appropriated, enthroned, idolised; he becomes little or nothing again. Like a l'archite.

After the Mass at Abu Ghosh, I drove with my family the eleven miles east to Jerusalem. There we visited the Church of the Holy Sepulchre, the very ground where the risen Christ had appeared to Mary Magdalene on this same day almost 2000 years ago and said more or less the same thing he said to the disciples at Emmaus: 'Do not hold onto me!' (Jn 2:11-18). Here Jesus chose to make himself visible to the most despised of sinners – a fallen woman – and to make her the premier evangelist of his risen message. Moreover, standing there on the spot where the gardener appeared to the Magdalene, I could not help recalling that what women prostitutes were in Jesus' time, the handicapped are all too often in our own day: scorned, spurned, unwelcomed – the lowest of the low.

Afterwards, as I wandered with my family through those narrow winding streets of Jerusalem, I realised it was in a closed room of this city that Jesus made his third apparition after his death: this time to the disciples (including the two just returned from Emmaus). Once again, we discover some of the simplest messages of L'Arche. The overcoming of fear: the apostles are so 'terrified' by what they see that they cannot recognise Jesus at first (Lk 24:35-48); they mistake him for a ghost. Doubts invade their hearts. But Jesus tells them not to be afraid – to approach and touch his wounds. And seeing that they are still 'disbelieving', still not accepting that his wounded body is risen from the dead, he resorts once more to the nourishment motif. 'Have you anything to eat?' And it is only when he takes some broiled fish and sits and eats with them that they finally recognise him. They see and hear his message of dying and rising again, a message that comes through the body, a broken body, bruised and hungry for something to eat. Through woundedness and want the divine makes itself known. As in L'Arche.

It was, however, when we drove north to Galilee the following day (a Monday) that I began to appreciate some deeper implications of the L'Arche vision of the Gospel. Visiting the fourth and last site where Jesus appeared after his death – the shore between Tabgha and Capernaum – I realised that the miracle of bread and fish was nothing less than the story of Christ himself – Christ as gift of food and life. The only trace now remaining is a fresco of two small loaves and fishes. The miracle of multiplication from next to nothing, the mystery of excess from paucity, of surplus from scarcity. The mystery of less as more.

Standing on the stony beach of Tabgha with my youngest daughter Sarah – who was busily collecting tiny shells (like mustard seeds from the sea) for her friends back in Dublin – I thought about the passage in question (Jn 21:1-14). When Jesus stood on this same spot on this same day two thousand years ago, his disciples 'did not know that it was Jesus'. And when he called across to them in their boat some ninety metres from shore, asking if they had any fish, and they said no, they still did not recognise him. It was only when he instructed them to cast their empty nets out the other side of the boat, resulting in the famous miraculous catch, that the most impetuous and unthinking of them all, Simon Peter, the very one who had denied him three times a few days earlier, finally recognised him, thanks to John, and jumped into the water!

Coming ashore, Peter and the other disciples found a charcoal fire already prepared for them, with fish and bread. 'Come and have breakfast', said Jesus. For he knew their hunger. He knew their want, their lack, their need, their desire. He invited them to sit and eat. As John writes: 'Now none of the disciples dared to ask him, "Who are you?" because they knew it was the Lord. Jesus came and took the bread and gave it to them, and did the same with the fish'.

So what's the message? Seen from a L'Arche point of view, the prophetic message of Christianity, inscribed in these four Paschal visitations, might go something like this:

If you are hungry and need to eat bread and fish, ask for it and you shall have your fill. If you see a lost loved one standing on the shore and are filled with joy, throw decorum to the wind, jump into the waves and swim to shore. If someone gives you food, do not ask for identity papers or credentials ('Who are you?'), just sit and receive. If you are wanting in body or mind – that is, handicapped – and your nets are still empty after many tries, do not despair; someone will come and tell you where to cast your net so that you may have life and have it more abundantly. What's more, the wonderful thing about this God of little things is that he gives with a gratuity that defies the limits of space and time. Now he's gone, now he's here, now he's gone again. Now he's dead, now he's alive. Now he's buried, now risen. Now the net is empty, now it's full. And more surprising still, the fish is cooked for us even before we get ashore and unload our nets! 'Come and have breakfast', Jesus says as the boat touches the land.

L'Arche reminds us, in short, of the post-Paschal message that the Kingdom of Heaven is given to fishermen and fallen women, to those lost and wandering on the road from Jerusalem to nowhere, to the wounded and weak and hungry, to those who lack and do not despair of their lack, to little people, to the 'poor in spirit'. Yes, L'Arche testifies that after the long night of fasting and waiting and darkness and need, afloat on a wilderness of sea, breakfast is always ready.

L'Arche is no temple. It floats and blesses all who sail in her. The followers of L'Arche, assistants and handicapped alike, possess little or nothing. They have nothing, they simply are. Just so they incarnate the message of Christ: Do not hold onto things! They let go. They let things be by being themselves.

As I returned with my family from the sea of Galilee to Jerusalem, we passed Mount Tabor, the hill where Jesus (shortly before his death this time) was transfigured in the sight of his disciples, instructing them afterwards to tell no one and to build no altars or temples in remembrance. Peering up at the huge basilica now perched on that hill, I felt how easy it is to compromise the Christian message by erecting triumphal monuments there where Christ himself asked for discretion, for nothing, at most a trace. And driving into Nazareth later that afternoon I thought how dispiriting it was to see Christians and Muslims fighting over who would appropriate the vast 'millennial' space in front of the Church of the Annunciation (a giant edifice now towering over the ground where a humble young woman once knelt). As dispiriting as it was to witness, the following day, the various Christian sects – Armenian, Greek Orthodox, Coptic and Catholic – skirmishing with silver thuribles and bronze crucifixes over rights of procession through the Church of the Nativity in Bethlehem.

Not that such violence is the prerogative of Christian zealots. Bitter conflicts over the possession of holy places are equally rife in the other revealed religions. The Jews with their Wailing Wall and the Muslims with their Dome of the Rock. Why such strife and hostility should continue to exist in the Holy City of Jerusalem – that messianic City on the Hill *par excellence* – as we approach the third millennium is a vexed question. Why the great monotheistic religions are still at war over the rock of Mount Moriah or the tomb of Abraham (in Hebron) is a depressing enigma.

All I knew for sure as I wandered through this ancient Holy Land was that I sensed the Holy One, not in the great monuments of power and triumph but in the silent, scattered ruins that still bear testimony – as only traces can – to things that come and go, like the still small voice, like the burning bush, like the voice crying in the wilderness, like the word made flesh, like the wind that blows where it wills. Or if I were to cite places: like the ruined walls of Capernaum where Jesus and the apostles took refuge after their expulsion from Nazareth; like the hill-caves of Sitve and Avdat where the Christian Napoteans (a people now extinct) rested on their passage through the Negev desert; or the sequestered hermitages of St George and Maar Saba carved into rockcliffs in the hills of Judaea. For these are places that resisted and still resist the triumphalism of ecclesiastical empire. Hide-outs, off the beaten track, without foundation. Cut against the grain. Self-effacing, modest, vulnerable, welcoming. Sanctuaries for migrants. Shelters for the exiled. Footholds for the forgotten. Arks. Perfect places for L'Arche communities. Cyphers, perhaps, of a new millennium?

PHILLIPE

Deaf and dumb since his hapless birth.
Inside the echo chamber of his skull
He hears the grimace of grinding teeth;
His form of broken, internal speech.
And always he lifts white, sightless eyes
Towards all pulsing sources of light, skies
That warm his insistent, upraised face,
Airs that play around his naked body,
Waters that pour, caress, and bless until
He breaks, like a bird, into grateful cries.
Handsome as some damaged Gothic angel,
Fate has yet left him one startling skill,
A lithe torso he arches with fakir's grace,
Which may not spare his early disappearance.

John Montague

Anne Gibson, married with three children, lives in Lisnaskea, Co Fermanagh. She is a solicitor by profession and an enthusiastic member of the Lisnaskea Faith and Light community. She first became involved in Faith and Light in 1987 and her ensuing friendship with people with learning disabilities changed her life. She is a practising Catholic and her faith and practice is an extremely important dimension in her life. She believes in the urgency of the mission of ecumenism within Faith and Light spirituality. She currently serves as National Coordinator of Faith and Light in Ireland and facilitates the International Ecumenical Commission for Faith and Light.

ENTERTAINING ANGELS – A FAITH AND LIGHT EXPERIENCE

Don't forget to show hospitality to strangers, for some who have done this have entertained angels without realising it!
(Heb 13:2)

Faith and Light is a non-residential community organisation, founded by Jean Vanier and Marie Helene Matthieu, which brings together people with learning disability, their families and those who would like to be their friends. We come together regularly, not as helpers and helped, but as friends, to build community and to provide friendship, acceptance and understanding in a Christian context.

Faith and Light originates from the same spiritual family as L'Arche and often describes itself as a sister of L'Arche. Both organisations are nourished by the same spirituality, which recognises as gift the qualities of littleness and humility. Family can provide support and love. And there is the added security in knowing that Faith and Light is not on its own when witnessing to the role of the vulnerable in a world that seems to proclaim a very different message with such volume and clamour that one tiny voice runs the risk of not being heard.

Just like L'Arche, Faith and Light also has a story that must be told. In the mid 1960s, a small family in France, Camille and Gerard Profit and their two profoundly handicapped sons, Loic and Thadee, felt a deep desire to go on pilgrimage to Lourdes. Loic and Thadee are unable to walk or talk, and need to be fed and clothed. Their means of communication is wordless, high pitched and piercing. Their parents are both now deceased but their sons are core members in L'Arche communities in Trosly, France, where Jean Vanier himself lives.

Back in the sixties, this family was told that their presence on the diocesan pilgrimage could cause problems for the other pilgrims. They travelled to Lourdes on their own and experienced rejection in the hotel and on the streets. They felt lonely and needed support and help from friends. They shared their story with Jean Vanier and a friend called Marie Helene Matthieu.

Jean Vanier had at this stage been involved in establishing L'Arche communities for four years, from 1964. Every year they had all gone on pilgrimage together and Jean had discovered that pilgrimages had helped the men and women with whom he lived to grow in their relationship with God and to develop an increasing awareness of Church. Marie Helene had been very much affected by the sufferings of parents and their desire that their sons and daughters should be fully integrated into the Church and into society. In 1968 a group of people met in Europe to plan a major pilgrimage to Lourdes, which would primarily be around people with mental handicap.

Over a three-year period, this pilgrimage was planned. During that time small groups of about thirty people met in their parishes every month to build bonds of friendship and community so that no one would feel alone. And on Holy Thursday, 1971, 12,000 pilgrims came from fifteen countries to celebrate the pain of Good Friday and the joy of Easter Sunday together. This was not a pilgrimage of isolated individuals but one of friendship and support, each pilgrim being part of a community of thirty or so, which included people with mental handicap, their families, their friends and their chaplain. For three days, we are told, they lived in incredible peace and joy. On Easter Monday morning, all gathered for a sending home ceremony and the cry was 'This cannot end'. Jean Vanier agreed and his response was 'Together with the handicapped people, do all that is inspired by the Holy Spirit to sustain these communities of love that surrounds them'.

No longer was the pilgrimage the incentive to meet in community, but in its place came the wish of the members to continue as before. And so Faith and Light was born. Jean Vanier himself expresses amazement at the growth of Faith and Light and believes strongly that the movement was inspired by the Holy Spirit at a time in the world when the weak and the vulnerable were being tossed aside by a society more interested in success and achievement than in the vulnerability and slow quietude that leads us into God's presence. At a time when our young people are being constantly pushed to strive for success, Faith and Light says that simply being with people with mental handicap can bring peace and fulfilment.

No faith group, age group, gender group or ability group is excluded from Faith and Light. There is a place for everyone, and input from everyone, even if it is only a simple smile, is considered a gift and is valued. This inclusivity is one of Faith and Light's strengths and beauties.

What do we do? Nothing world shattering! We are non-residential communities of young friends (usually teenagers), older friends, people with mental handicap, and their families. Each community is spiritually accompanied by another essential member, the chaplain, who also fulfils the role of friend. We meet every month, we share together, pray together and enjoy ourselves. Like Mary in the Mary and Martha story, we 'be' together, we take time to listen to each other's story and to discover the person behind the label. Thus we open up a new dimension of life for each other. Some of our members cannot use words to pray, so we use actions, mime, music, picture and symbol when we give praise to God. Outside of the main monthly gathering, friendship is built up between members through phonecalls, meeting for a chat and through going together on regional or national pilgrimages, national holidays and other organised events.

Faith and Light enables the whole family to come together. It enables parents to meet other parents and to talk with them about their child, to meet new friends who have time to listen and can offer support when times are difficult. It enables brothers and sisters to meet other siblings who have a handicapped brother or sister too. It enables families who do not have a handicapped child to discover a way of living the gospel that they would never have imagined. Faith and Light believes that these communities must be firmly integrated in their relevant parish community – then they find themselves at the heart of Church, where they rightfully belong.

Anyone who is familiar with the writings and the vision of Jean Vanier will know something of the spirituality of Faith and Light. The Beatitudes, which Christ first preached in the Sermon on the Mount, have become a very important touchstone in terms of that spirituality. If we live the Beatitudes, then we are living Faith and Light, because in a way Faith and Light is a beatitude. In the Beatitudes, those whom many people in our society would consider weak and inadequate are exalted and given their rightful dignity as individuals, created in God's image. Faith and Light endeavours to do the same. Our society is inclined to celebrate the young, the strong, the beautiful, the intelligent, the healthy, the wealthy. Christ celebrated the weak, the leper, the marginalised, the sinner, the broken in body and spirit, and the poor. He continues to challenge us to do likewise. In Faith and Light we are given the opportunity to meet that challenge and, in doing so, we quickly learn the truth of weakness and brokenness in our own hearts and minds.

I have been privileged for twelve years to be a member of a Faith and Light community in Lisnaskea, Co Fermanagh, and to have friends who are handicapped in their capacity to learn. I am a wife and a mother of three. I work as a solicitor with my husband in a small family practice. I suppose I was in the mainstream of life with success as the main goal, and then Faith and Light introduced me to people with mental handicap. Gradually they have turned my world upside down. And the writings and teachings of Jean Vanier, inspired by his friendship with people with mental handicap, have given me a new way of looking at the world, at people and at my faith.

In my world of work there must be value for money, people demand satisfaction – a case won, a marriage ended. These are different worlds with different realities and it's difficult to build bridges between these two worlds. But Faith and Light has taught me time and again that it is only in humility, in peace, in silence, that a heart can know a truth.

Jean Vanier talks about the need for adults to build barriers and defences around themselves to protect them from being too vulnerable, from being hurt. He often talks about the need we all have to hide the little child deep down inside of us, who is continually calling out for acceptance and praise and affirmation and love. Faith and Light offers a chance to each one of us to recognise and own that little voice which is hoping that others will like us just as we are. Over the years in Faith and Light I have begun to touch truth in a more meaningful way than ever before. The first lesson I learned was from parents, about relationship.

Parents in Faith and Light taught me how really to love my own children unconditionally, without wanting them to do things my way, to be the way I wanted them to be. I saw the unconditional love that parents had for their child with mental handicap, their total acceptance of them just as they were, and I asked myself, 'Do I love my children just as they are, or do I put conditions on my love? I'll love you if you do things my way and become what I want you to become.' And in answering those questions, I gradually began to discover the true meaning of relationship. I feel that parents in Faith and Light taught me to give my three children the freedom to be themselves and to make their mistakes and to know they were loved. I learned I had to die to myself and to my ambitions in order to give true life to my children and to allow them to be just as God had given them to me.

Some months ago I remember having a conversation with a mother of a young lad with multiple disabilities and she was relaying a conversation she had had the previous day with a woman who couldn't believe that she was still getting up a couple of times during the night to her eighteen-year-old son. She shook her head in amazement and said 'Some people haven't a clue'. And it's true – the need for care is absolute, total, unconditional, consistent and forever ongoing.

Sometimes it can be tempting, when we talk about Faith and Light in public, to concentrate on the joy, the love, the lack of inhibition, the fun we have together. It's tempting to glamorise, to gloss over the reality of the pain and suffering that exists alongside the joy and the fun. People with mental handicap have their difficult times too and they can be very demanding – like us all! The unconditional love that is demanded from parents and family, the tediousness and exhaustion that comes from caring twenty-four hours a day, seven days a week, the very real need for respite and support – none of these things should be hidden or forgotten. Faith and Light teaches us about the necessity to remain true to the pain, walk with it, own it.

I feel privileged to have touched on the courage and selflessness of parents in Faith and Light. They are powerful examples to society of what it is to love others truly; their lives speak so loudly of the real meaning of commitment in a world where such a word is no longer very relevant. The work that they do is rarely appreciated by the State, by the Church or by society in general. My experience over the last twelve years in Faith and Light has led me to believe that they are among the silent heroes of this millennium.

We often have the privilege of sharing in the pain of mothers and fathers. It is only rarely we glimpse the pain of the one with handicap. So I really want to tell you a story about a young girl whom we'll call Josephine. Josephine finds it difficult to speak and to walk, but she is always so full of joy and has brought such happiness to her family and her community.

A few years ago, Josephine, her mother and myself attended a five-day Inter-Church Retreat led by Jean Vanier. We spent a lot of time together. On the night before it finished we joined in an evening of reconciliation. We took part in a very profound and touching Way of the Cross. There was an almost tangible atmosphere of sadness and sorrow. Afterwards we all had a chance to go to a priest for the sacrament of reconciliation, or to a minister for prayer and a blessing, or just to share.

The three of us decided, on Josephine's suggestion, that we would go for prayer and a blessing to Rev. Ruth Patterson, a Presbyterian minister who works in the ministry of healing and reconciliation in Belfast. She was also participating in the Retreat. When we returned to our seats, we were silent and all three in prayer. And then in that silence, Josephine began to sob. We both automatically embraced her, trying to shield her from the sorrow she was feeling. Then she said, very slowly: 'It's hard sometimes.' Her mother explained to me afterwards that they often have these times of heartbreak together.

This young girl is such a source of life and fun in her community, her smiles and her hugs bring such warmth to us all. I could never have guessed at the deep down pain she feels from time to time. I was privileged to glimpse, for a precious moment, the pain of those with handicap. Josephine allowed me to see her pain, alive, and present in her. As Christians, we all believe that Jesus lives in each one of us. That moment I was enabled to know at heart level that Jesus lives in Josephine, with all his pain and all his joy, with all his wisdom and in all his vulnerability. That was an eternity moment for me. A sacred moment of deep truth.

> One day some parents brought their children to Jesus so he could touch them and bless them, but the disciples told them not to bother him. But when Jesus saw what was happening, he was very displeased with his disciples. He said to them, 'Let the children come to me. Don't stop them! For the Kingdom of God belongs to such as these. I assure you, anyone who doesn't have their kind of faith will never get into the Kingdom of God.' Then he took the children into his arms and placed his hands on their heads and blessed them. (Mk 10:13-16)

This Scripture quotation is very central to the ethos of Faith and Light. These are powerful words with dire implications for all of us. People with mental handicap have no pride. They are humble, loving, needing, asking others for love, reaching down into the little bit of goodness in all of us, challenging us – just as Jesus does. Just as in L'Arche, Faith and Light also sometimes describes those with mental handicap as the silent prophets of today's world. Prophets in the Old Testament were people with a mission to bring back the wandering, wayward people to the healing presence of their God. In Faith and Light we come across many stories of how those with mental handicap have brought people who are termed 'normal' in today's world back to the basic truth of how to live a Christian life.

In Faith and Light we discover that it is through those little prophets at the heart of our Faith and Light communities that God can speak to us of his love and acceptance of us just as we are, of his compassion and pain, of his joy and celebration, of his welcome and invitation to follow him.

One summer, at a Faith and Light Summer Holiday, Anne taught me the true meaning of compassion. She cried a lot that week and I began by trying to make everything better for her. I failed miserably, nothing seemed to work. Then I began to feel frustrated, I really wanted her to enjoy this holiday. If Anne had been a friend whom society labels 'normal' she would have pretended she was happy, just to please me, but Anne would have none of that. Slowly I began to realise that I couldn't make it better, there was no solution to this problem. I simply knew that I should just walk quietly with her in whatever her pain was. And then we were both able to relax and be at peace in each other's company. We were friends. Prior to that holiday I thought I knew the meaning of compassion, but I merely knew a definition of the word. Anne taught me, at heart level, the true meaning of compassion, a lesson that has had far-reaching consequences in my relationship with many people since.

At one of our recent Fiestas, we mimed the story of the Prodigal Son. Frank played Dad and Jimmy played the bad son! The story was explained to them both and they were told how important it would be for them really to hug each other when the son returned. Now if we had some of our other 'normal' members playing the parts, inhibitions and shyness would have totally ruined the profound meeting, but Frank and Jimmy hugged the life out of each other with such delight; it is an image of reconciliation that will stay with all who saw it for a long time.

And, of course, we have a Faith and Light Christmas party celebration every year. I remember very clearly, at one of these parties, having a conversation with a mother who told me how her beautiful daughter related to her that morning the story of a dream she had had the night before:

> … Mary and Joseph were in the dream and there was a beautiful light and they made the star to shine on me.

Such a beautiful image and such an affirmation of all we proclaim in Faith and Light. We are always amazed at how those with mental handicap can speak or represent a truth so simply. All the dross of words and philosophy and theology is stripped away and we are left with the simple smile of welcome, the hug of reconciliation, the pure cleansing of innocent tears, the need to treat all God's creatures with love and respect and dignity. Yes, they do point the way for us, they are continually the stars that guide us to where Jesus is.

Jesus came into this world as a tiny vulnerable baby, handicapped by his great love for us, and his greatest desire was to teach us how to love and serve one another and thus to help us discover his peace. His last prayer recorded in John's Gospel was:

> My prayer for all of them is that they will be one, just as you and I are one, Father, that as you are in me and I am in you so they will be in us, and the world may believe you sent me. (Jn 17:21)

In 1971 Faith and Light began as a pilgrimage to Lourdes, but even at that early beginning, there were people from other Christian Churches who joined the pilgrimage. Over the years Faith and Light has become a world-wide association, which has embraced people from all Christian traditions and all faiths. It has been given an ecumenical mission. Now, in 1999, there are eighty-nine countries where Faith and Light witnesses to the gifts of people who have a mental handicap, with members who are rooted securely in different Church traditions and in different faiths:

> Faith and Light does not wish to be another Church; it wants to help each person discover the beauty and the gift of the Church which brought them into being and of which they are a part.
> (*Ecumenism in Faith and Light*, p. 16)

The needs of those who are part of our Faith and Light communities had to be addressed, and Faith and Light, although born on Catholic soil, gradually began to realise its ecumenical mission. Faith and Light was challenged to accept and to serve the spiritual needs of people from a wide diversity of traditions. Faith and Light is learning, little by little, through experience and through friendship, through listening and through deep respect of difference. Most important to Faith and Light is that each person be encouraged to remain true to their own Church and remain securely rooted in the soil that has nurtured the expression of their faith.

There are twenty-six communities of Faith and Light in Ireland, five of which are in their first formative years. All of them are Catholic. This is not by choice, it is simply the way of it. But seeds are being sown in Ireland and we are hopeful that we will soon be welcoming communities that will open up to us the richness of other traditions, which we have missed out on heretofore:

> Faith and Light believes in the grace and presence of Jesus in each Church. Faith and Light also believes that people with mental handicap have a mission to help different Churches in their step towards unity.
> (*Ecumenism in Faith and Light*, p.12)

In Faith and Light, by simply being with people with mental handicap, we learn about poverty of spirit, humility, openness, welcome. We learn that difference is not threatening but enriching; we learn to say 'I accept you as you are'. We learn to live as equals, recognising each other's gifts, affirming each other. All these lessons open our hearts to the possibility of acceptance of those who are different, not only different in ability but also different in ways of worship, different in Church tradition, different in ecclesiastical beliefs. It suddenly becomes obvious that God is Father of us all and that he does not use labels when feeding his sheep. The following very beautiful quotation is from the Charter of Faith and Light:

> … lack of humility and simplicity of heart is probably the principal spiritual obstacle to communion in spirit and in truth of all those who believe in Jesus. Those who are wounded in their intelligence by the very radiance of their poverty, lead Christians of different denominations into the beatitude of poverty of heart and thus allow them to rediscover the spirit of God.

My tentative incursions into the area of ecumenism in the company of those with mental handicap have taught me that ecumenism is not about making people the same but rather it is about respecting the right of each person to be different. Within any family there can be differences and yet there can be unity; within any Faith and Light community there are differences and yet we strive all the time for unity because that is the greatest desire in the heart of those around whom we build community. It is the need for acceptance, the need for communion, love and friendship that our friends with mental handicap challenge us to deal with constantly. They underline the urgent desire of that last prayer that Jesus prayed to his Father after illustrating his love for his disciples with a dramatic act of simple humility when he washed their feet and told them they must 'go and do likewise'.

I was privileged to be part of the Irish delegation to the Faith and Light International Meeting in Quebec in July 1998. This meeting takes place every four years and brings together delegates from all the communities all over the world to be renewed in the vision and mission of Faith and Light in today's world. At that meeting, Marie Helene Matthieu, one of our founders, described

Faith and Light as a 'tiny flame of love in a world of war and division'. Two weeks after arriving home one of the most horrendous events in the recent troubled period of war and division in Northern Ireland happened. On 15 August 1998, the small town of Omagh was shattered when that community was subjected to abject suffering and devastation. A car bomb exploded in the busy market town on that Saturday afternoon, killing thirty people and maiming and disabling many more for a lifetime.

There is a Faith and Light community in Omagh and one of our families was among those who were so tragically bereaved. At the beginning of September the northern region of Faith and Light met together for a day of pilgrimage, prayer and celebration as we do every year. That family and one other bereaved family whose friends had invited them along, joined us. They were very fragile and broken. Why did they come? Because they knew that Faith and Light was a safe place where they could experience comfort and support and where they would find people prepared to walk with them in their pain. That is what Faith and Light can do best, be with people in pain. And that day, Marie Helene's words literally took flesh. Faith and Light became a tiny vulnerable flame of love in their dark world for a time.

There is a peace in Faith and Light which helps us to discover our hearts, our real selves. We have an opportunity to learn to co-operate rather than to compete, to do with rather than do for. In a society where we are constantly being barraged by the media and by advertising in general about the importance of striving for success, beauty, health, wealth, it has been our experience in Faith and Light that people with mental handicap call us gently back to the priorities of the Beatitudes. In a society where commitment does not mean very much anymore, parents of people with mental handicap have the potential to give strong witness to the depth of the meaning of that word. In a world that is being bombarded with news of indiscriminate killings in schools and colleges; where ethnic cleansing policies are given credence and authority by governments of European and African countries, we need people who cry out to us for love, in order that our civilisation holds on to qualities of sensitivity, care and compassion and in order to preserve as sacrosanct society's almost forgotten belief in the dignity of humankind.

At a Faith and Light gathering, we experience warmth, acceptance, smiles, hugs, suffering and pain, delight in meeting again, the pure joy of clapping and singing, the simple interpretation of the Gospels in mime. These are all qualities that have enriched the essence of my life. Faith and Light has introduced me to a world where Jesus is very much alive and patiently waiting to be recognised, understood and loved. In Faith and Light we become more and more aware of the privilege and blessing we receive when we dare to entertain angels.

DOWN'S SYNDROME GOD

The little boy circles beneath the trees
That circle the field.

Now and again he dashes onto the grass,
Takes sudden fright, runs off to hide again.

The children are busy with football,
Games of run and chase.

He fears their shouting,
He cannot tell whether they will welcome him.

His heart is full of love;
If they but knew their need.

Pádraig G. Daly

John Gibson is one of Ireland's leading pianist composers. Since 1982 he has been Senior Lecturer at the Cork School of Music and has performed widely in concerto, recital and chamber music concerts, often featuring his own compositions. His music has been heard in Japan, America, England, France, Germany, Russia, Romania and Israel, and on stage, radio and television in Ireland. His recordings include Aislingí Ceoil, Reflections on the Water, Out of Ireland, Volume *and* Contemporary Irish Piano Music. *He has been a friend of the L'Arche community in Cork for the past ten years.*

WALKING DOWN THE LADDER

The feature I find most attractive about the spirituality of L'Arche is that the stone which the builder rejected has become the cornerstone. Jean Vanier, who founded L'Arche over thirty years ago, expounds eloquently on this revolutionary gospel teaching. So it is not just that residents in L'Arche are well cared for but that residents and assistants share everyday life together in a daily exchange of each other's gifts. Sharing good times and bad, but in a commitment to be there for each other.

I have known L'Arche for over ten years. I'm a friend of the community in Cork and the community is a very good friend to me. So I enjoy visiting the various houses, sharing dinner and the wash-up with residents, assistants and other friends who take part in the life of the community. With regard to wash-up, this is very often an occasion for singing, jokes and storytelling. In fact I have discovered a new family, sharing birthdays, arrivals and departures and wonderful intimate Masses and prayer in a setting that is open, faithful and forgiving. I can't imagine my life without the characters of the community. I have been witness to gentle miracles where people who have been institutionalised for years, sometimes decades, have unfolded and revealed their many gifts of personality, be it through singing, reciting or, in some cases, through a phenomenal recalling of dates and events. I remember Marie Deasy coming to L'Arche for the first time. She was almost totally silent except for some mutterings and inward sounds. Today she talks, has a great sense of humour and sings Irish ballads beautifully. To see the transformation is striking and to share her company at mealtimes is a treat.

I am also reminded of Joe McKenna from L'Arche whom I first met about ten years ago. He is one of the founder members of Suaimhneas, the second house in the Cork community. It's fair to say that Joe is generally talking from morning to night! He is full of energy and has to be reminded from time to time that he has already told a particular story perhaps three or four times! For some reason I got on very well with Joe from the start and we never fight or argue. So much so that Joe reminds me regularly 'We never fight', 'We Dubs stick together' and 'Tell them about Kerry'. The latter remark refers to a holiday I went on with L'Arche to Kerry some years ago. We went to a house in Rathmore. Joe was cooking dinner one day and I was helping. Joe was making hamburgers, when a group of French visitors from L'Arche arrived unexpectedly. Panic stations! We hadn't enough food, so Joe gave everyone a small dinner, sharing what we had and also making lots of jelly. Now Joe loves to tell everyone, especially in my presence, the modern parable of the loaves and fishes: the burgers and the jelly!

Joe is also a musician. He busks in Cork city and sings and plays guitar wonderfully out of tune! He has a regular spot where, because of his warmth and good nature, local restaurants provide him with food and drink whenever he is performing. He has a wonderful collection of songs and hymns and Christmas carols which he belts out with great gusto, and this provides him with extra funds and an independence that is valuable.

Let me tell you the story of Joe's hamster, Josephine. Josephine was the last in a long list of pets who came to an unhappy end, for one reason or another. I volunteered to look after Josephine when Joe was away on holidays. Now, while feeding her, I foolishly left her cage door open. Of course she escaped, making a new home behind one of my kitchen cupboards. For over a week I tried to set live traps for Josephine, without success. Every morning she would have managed to dodge the trap and carry off the food inside. As Joe's return was imminent I was getting desperate. I tried staying up some of the night to catch her, with no success. Eventually a member of the community remembered reading a *Reader's Digest* article on how to capture escaped hamsters!

The plan was to drape a towel soaked in apple juice down the side of a bucket, into which one placed pieces of apple. I decided to make sure Josephine wouldn't escape, should she fall for the trap, by coating the base and sides of the bucket with vegetable oil. My efforts were only too successful! Josephine stood shivering the next day in the bucket, covered in oil! I was desperate; how could I clean her coat? I brought her to the House of Prayer (An Cuan) where an assistant gently washed her oil-matted hair. Unfortunately, later that day Josephine had to be put down by the vet. Soon afterwards, Joe said to me, 'God won't hold it against you', and months later when I had forgotten this sorry saga, Joe again reminded me with gentleness not to bathe any of his pets when looking after them! We still haven't fought, and again Joe reminds me that even if we did, we would still be friends. I'm happy to have Joe as a friend, not just because he is lively, cheerful and gifted, but because in his openness, he shows the way life can be with warmth and forgiveness.

Another friend who embodied the spirit of L'Arche for me, although she was not a member of the community, was Maureen Forde. She shared the lively faith journey of L'Arche through attending retreats in Switzerland and Ireland. I met Maureen first on a weekend organised by the Focolare movement in Maynooth back in the eighties. We shared meals and chats during the Mariapolis. The weekend was very enjoyable and friendly, and Maureen and I became great friends over the succeeding years. At that stage, because of MS, Maureen was walking with the aid of crutches. Unfortunately there was no remission during the rest of her life. Throughout the time I knew her the one word I associate with her is 'marvellous', which was her usual response as to how she was. In spite of the dark days Maureen radiated a warmth and light that attracted friends from all over Europe and Australia. She took great delight in celebrating life.

I remember we went on a retreat given by Jean Vanier in

Maynooth in 1992 and, although in a wheel chair, indeed perhaps because of it, as well as her radiant personality, she was never without helpers and friends. We shared a great interest in music and in faith matters. She had a lovely saying on her table at home in Raheny, 'There is nothing I cannot do today, with God'.

Being with Maureen was regularly a laugh and a tonic. All her friends revelled in her wit, good humour and winking ability! So whether it was being wheeled up Grafton Street eating jelly babies, or enjoying afternoon tea at the Shelbourne at Christmas, she broke the bread of her life abundantly and shared herself with many. She was a profound gift in my life and even when totally debilitated by her illness, she still communicated with her eyes and her wink and gave life to many. Her parents, Dorothy and Mike, who cared for and loved their daughter so courageously, included the following prayer on her memorial card; one that Maureen prayed over and over again:

> I asked for strength that I might achieve,
> He made me weak that I might obey.
> I asked for health that I might do greater things,
> I was given grace that I might do better things.
>
> I asked for riches that I might be happy,
> I was given poverty that I might be wise.
> I asked for power that I might have praise,
> I was given weakness that I might feel the need of God.
> I asked for all things that I might enjoy life,
> I was given life that I might enjoy all things.
>
> I received nothing that I asked for,
> All that I hoped for.
>
> My prayer was answered.

The transparency of Maureen's personality and faith was a wonder to behold. In spite of her disability and, perhaps, because of it, she gave so much to us all and was attentive to those who had the privilege of sharing her presence. She remains a light to us all, having been very much grounded in the reality of her own humanity.

The House of Prayer in the L'Arche community in Cork is very special. The oratory is in the lovely garden and has as its centrepiece a bog-oak tabernacle. So the real presence of the Lord is present for the community night or day. To witness Angela's outpouring of prayer or Donie's prayer for peace in Northern Ireland at the regular Tuesday night prayer, is to witness the direct, prophetic language of the Bible. It comes from the heart and goes to the heart and soul. To be present is to be humbled. I'm sure the late spiritual writer and L'Arche priest Henri Nouwen must have felt the call to L'Arche through such outpourings. His colleagues belittled his exit from successful academic life to live daily with those with learning disabilities. In one of his last books he describes movingly how, when he joined the L'Arche community at Daybreak in Toronto, he was given Adam to care for. Now Adam was the most fragile member of the house and Henri felt he was the most inadequate person to be in such a role. The gradual unfolding of the relationship is beautiful and Henri learnt from Adam how best to be present to him.

Jean Vanier's writings, in particular *Treasures of the Heart* (my favourite spiritual book – a tiny book of short reflections), are my food for the journey and for daily reflection. I keep coming back to the message of the good news in them, and I like particularly Jean's concept of walking down the ladder of life. This doesn't mean refusing to achieve and to be creative with our various gifts, but walking down the ladder to meet our fellow humans, to accompany them and be present to them. There's a wonderful fresco in Monte Cassino by Pietro Annigoni and it portrays someone with one hand to the ear, listening. The title of the fresco is *Obedience*! What a wonderful description of attentiveness, of being present in this world of hurry and rush. To stand still and be present to the gift of whoever we encounter in the present moment. This is what Vanier means, I think; to be grounded in the present moment and break the bread of life with whomever we've been sent.

One of the most beautiful recent experiences of this sacrament of the present moment occurred for me during a recent trip to Compiègne in northern France. A group from Cork travelled to France to celebrate the tenth anniversary of the ordination of Fr Philip Kearney (Tim's brother). I was on my own for the last day of the trip and I wandered along to one of the L'Arche houses. I was invited to stay for a *goûter*, which turned out to be a birthday celebration for Joelle, one of the residents. The whole feast of birthday cake and Coca-Cola and juice was so relaxed and happy that it made a strong impression on me of peaceful communion and celebration. In Ireland today, where we are in danger of 'throwing the baby out with the bath water', spiritually speaking, I feel it is very important to slow down the Celtic Tiger mentality to discover again the presence of God in the present moment, and experience again the one hundred thousand welcomes of our island.

Perhaps in our prosperity and our striving, in a never-ending spiral of work, success and alienation, we've lost something of our warmth and welcome. I like the L'Arche concept of walking down the ladder to ground level. To be grounded in reality and to be in relationship with people instead of on the high wire, fleeing from true contact with one another and seeking comfort and support from that which only leads to loneliness. To learn to be in touch with the reality of our fellow humans and to understand how much we share in common is, for me, the ultimate challenge on our journey through life. Of course, we must live and develop our gifts, but opening the door of our hearts and sharing the broken bread of our humanity are what build community in the broadest sense, and this is what happens, on a daily basis, in L'Arche.

To conclude, I would say that L'Arche and its spirituality have been a great gift in my life over the past ten years or so. I call those who live in L'Arche my friends. I see people, not handicap. I witness freedom of expression, not barriers. I experience warmth, wit, good humour and directness of communication. I also see a space that we all need where people can develop their gifts and be supported in those areas where support is needed. This happens in L'Arche and we need to find the opening for it to happen in everyday life. People are being transformed in L'Arche and I think we can be too.

THEE

Weddings first and then christenings and then funerals.
It's as straightforward as subject, verb, object.
This move from the altar to the font to the mortuary chapel.
How it leaves us speechless, how it takes our breath away!
Yet the day I helped to carry my brother's coffin
There was the sound of confetti under my desert boots,
And after the worst two years since our records began,
The cot has come out of our attic like a Jew after a pogrom.
Amid all the bloodshed, we are one flesh assuming it,
At a standstill certainly, uncertainly, but still standing.

At the time of writing, the garden is dead and buried.
But come whenever, Passover say, or at Pentecost,
The kids will be playing Mass with their chocolate buttons,
Inventing miracle stories out of the telephone book
Where the ivy has gone and greened the cable for Cable TV
And the blackbird returns to her nest with a drinking straw from a
    Coke;
And I will be there, observing their serving, giving thanks
For our dying days in the land of the living; thanksgiving
For this indefinite time, this world, this definite article
Pronounced like the ancient form of a pronoun that stands for you.

Aidan Mathews

Tim Kearney graduated from University College, Dublin, in 1982 with a masters degree in Anglo-Irish literature. He taught literature and lectured on a part-time basis in the Anglo-Irish Department of UCD and at All Hallows College, Dublin, for two years. He lived and worked in the L'Arche community of Trosly-Breuil from 1982 to 1984. He became Founding Director of the L'Arche community in Cork in 1984. In 1996 he became the Regional Co-Ordinator of L'Arche in Ireland. He has worked on the editorial board of The Crane Bag *journal as well as* The Letters of L'Arche. *He has written widely on L'Arche and on issues of contemporary spirituality, and has led retreats in recent years. He is married to Maria and they live in Cork with their three children and are members of the L'Arche community.*

THE UPSIDE-DOWN KINGDOM

In my first year in L'Arche, I lived with a woman called Edith, who had a profound learning disability, in the community of Trosly-Breuil in France. She had been institutionalised for many years before coming to L'Arche and she knew the pain of rejection by her family and the anguish of loneliness. Edith's violence was that of self-mutilation. She would suddenly, and without forewarning, start to scream and to bang her fist fiercely against her forehead. She did this to such an extent that there was a gaping crater of raw and exposed flesh on her forehead. Her wound was heavily bandaged to protect her and she was given a crash-helmet to prevent her from hitting the rest of her head and skull. Even so, she would still bang her head violently against the nearest wall whenever the opportunity arose. I was very struck by the perceptive comment made by the community's psychiatrist at a case-conference for Edith, when he remarked that the physical pain incurred by her self-mutilation was easier for her to live with than the inner pain of her own emptiness and anguish, linked with her rejection and her broken self-image. Her inner pain must have been very great indeed.

I was equally struck during that first year I spent in L'Arche by some of the assistants who lived with Edith, particularly by their ability to stay with her in her moments of pain, sometimes physically holding and containing her, until her anguish had passed like a storm and a sense of calm returned to her features. I could see that there was something very healing for Edith in knowing that there were people in her life who were not afraid to be with her, and be there for her, in her moments of pain. I wondered where these assistants got the inner strength to be present to Edith in this way, as I could see that it was not an easy or comfortable space for them to be in. I realised just how much I had to learn and to grow if I were to be able to follow their example and do likewise myself one day.

One of the popular misconceptions about L'Arche is that it is a sort of Utopian community where jubilant beings lead a life of happy togetherness in an environment of peace and harmony, where singing and hugging and hand-clapping are the order of the day, Alleluia! Needless to say, this is something of a caricature. In some ways, nothing could be further from the truth. L'Arche, as a community, is a very real place. It is a place of hard realities and often painful struggles.

L'Arche is a place where human suffering is present in a visible and audible and often unpredictable way. This suffering is that of the people with learning disabilities whom we welcome, but it is, also, significantly, the pain of the assistants who chose to work with them and share their life. Being close to people in pain inevitably brings one in touch with one's own pain and this is never a comfortable experience. There is also the reality of conflict. Conflict is not something confined to the rows and quibbles that can often occur between our 'core members', that is to say, those with learning disabilities in our community. It is experienced at all levels of community life, between 'core members' and 'assistants', between the assistants themselves and, equally, between the different people in roles of leadership in the community. Conflict can be a draining and often destructive reality, and the hurt that it gives rise to is experienced in all its facets in the day-to-day life of a L'Arche community.

Another difficult reality in L'Arche, in particular for the assistants who live and work there, is the constant and relentless 'busyness' of life. This results in large part from L'Arche's dual identity as both a faith community on the one hand, and as a service provider for people with learning disabilities on the other. This dual identity, operating within the demanding context of an international network of communities (each one of which requires high levels of support and supervision), generates an enormous workload, which is really the work of two organisational structures rolled into one.

Given the intensity of living so close to the bone of human suffering and to the tensions of interpersonal conflict, not to mention the never-ending 'busyness' of life, it is hardly surprising to realise that the risk of burnout in L'Arche is very real. In this regard, L'Arche and, by extension, community life in general, can be a difficult, even dangerous, journey upon which to embark.

But if L'Arche is a place of risk and struggle, it is also a place of grace and personal growth, a place where one can be in touch with the mystery of life, in a real and intimate way.

I want in this article to share something of the struggle of living in L'Arche, but also something of the mystery that I have discovered hidden like a treasure in the field of this reality. This mystery can only be expressed in the language of paradox, in the upside-down logic of God's kingdom. In particular, I wish to focus on three realities of life in L'Arche that carry within them this element of paradox. Firstly, the reality of human suffering and pain, which contains within it the seeds of healing. Secondly, the reality of discovering a common humanity and a sense of belonging with those who are significantly different to me, both core members and assistants, and with whom I can often be in conflict, living and working at such close quarters. Thirdly, the reality of discovering, and of being nourished by, a vibrant spirituality in the midst of a busy and demanding way of life.

Suffering and the Healing Process

I have been taught much about the reality of human suffering by my brothers and sisters with a learning disability in L'Arche. The pain of people with learning disabilities is very real.

I am reminded of my friend Danny, a man with a learning disability in my own community in Cork. Though a very capable and gifted person in many ways, Danny is gripped at times by a very deep sense of anger and of anguish. At such moments he has a tendency to lose rational control of his actions and to flip into irrational and aggressive behaviour. His major handicap is secondary rather than primary, that is to say, linked with his volatile mood swings and broken self-image, rather than with his learning disability. In his moments of deep anguish and hurt, Danny often cries out: 'Why did God put me on this earth?' This is the pain of being a disappointment from the moment you are born, and of feeling unwanted.

Then growing up and going to a special school, as Danny has shared with me, and being teased on your way there and back by other 'normal' children telling you that you're 'a spastic' and that you're 'mad'. The pain of rejection in a world that values knowledge, power and social status, when you have few, if any, of these attributes and graces. Danny knows the reality of such pain.

Just as Danny is intimately acquainted with the reality of his own hurt and anguish, which can propel him at times into outbursts of anger and violent temper tantrums, he is also sensitive to the pain of others. He is a man who has compassion for those who suffer. He often prays for those who are having 'a hard time', including the homeless men and women – often refugees from Romania and elsewhere in Eastern Europe – whom he sees sleeping rough on Patrick's Street in Cork City. He is a peace-maker who abhors conflict and war in the world and, though from a nationalist background and culture, I have heard him pray for the family of a British soldier killed in Northern Ireland, that they be comforted in their pain and loss. He often prays for peace in the world. Whilst he loves flags and national emblems and is a passionate collector of same, he abhors borders, which divide human beings from each other. Though capable of anger and violence, Danny is a man capable of great gentleness, who loves children and who is naturally gifted with them. Danny is a person who is gifted in many ways on the level of the heart, and he has taught me much about what it means to be human.

I am fascinated by the fact that there is no specific word in the Irish language for someone with a learning disability. *Duine le Dia,* the term that is used, literally means 'a person linked to, or with God', someone who is 'wrapped up' in God. Danny is no saint and is someone whom people can find very difficult, at times impossible, to live with. He is often wrapped up, not in God, but in himself and his own preoccupations and concerns, and will complain, frequently, about how difficult it is to live and work in community. But there are times when he is also wrapped up in, and absorbed by, God. When he prays in the morning in our Workshop, sitting in the circle around the candle, he can sometimes be quite inspired. His face, instead of being tense and twisted with anguish, can radiate peace. Recently he prayed 'we don't know how lucky we are to live in a community... not like the people from Romania sleeping rough in Patrick's Street... we have food and a roof over our heads, we have work and we have friends... we should be thanking God and not complaining!'

Danny is my friend, and my brother in community. He is also a prophetic voice in my life, which I can hear, at certain moments, speaking words that both comfort and challenge me. He is, for me, a signpost of God's presence in the world.

Through the friendship and love he has experienced in his life in community, and through the faithful support of his parents, a slow healing has been taking place in Danny's heart. It is a healing that grows from Danny's awareness that there are significant others in his life who know his shadow side and still love him nonetheless, and who are willing to pay the often heavy cost of being there for him, and with him, in his pain. This experience of people being close to him in his suffering and not running away, but rather staying with him, showing him patience and compassion as well as challenge and discipline, gives Danny a strong sense of security. He knows that there are people around him who trust him and in whom he can place his trust. Trust, in so many ways, is at the heart of the healing process. Much of the work of L'Arche is about creating an atmosphere and an environment of trust, which enables this healing and growth to happen.

Today Danny knows that he is loved and accepted for who he is, in his light and in his darkness, in his strength and in his fragility, in his abilities and in his needs. Though Danny still struggles on an almost daily basis with self-doubt and feelings of rejection, and still requires high levels of support for his behaviour, which is still frequently challenging, he continues to grow as a person and to experience healing.

What are the essential aspects of the healing process that people like Edith and Danny and others experience in L'Arche? There are three key elements that I would identify: the human dimension; the professional dimension; and the spiritual dimension.

Firstly, the human dimension of the healing process in L'Arche is predicated on the option of 'being with' rather than 'doing for', which is another way of saying that friendship is more important than charity for people like Edith and Danny.

In L'Arche we endeavour to relate to the person with a learning disability, not as an object of care or therapy, but as a subject, as a full and complete human being, in his or her own right. This is expressed, first and foremost, in the fact that assistants in our L'Arche houses are invited to come and to share life with our core members, not, primarily, to work for them. It is in this sharing of life, as with brothers and sisters in the same family, with all the intensity and struggle as well as fulfilment and growth that this entails, which is the hallmark of L'Arche. To choose to share your life with someone is one of the greatest statements you can make in terms of valuing and affirming them.

The most difficult and challenging aspect of this 'being with' in L'Arche is when it involves 'being with' those like Danny and Edith, who are hurting. This is an uncomfortable and demanding experience for the assistants, because it puts them in touch with their own pain. It is this choice to stay with my own discomfort, as I remain present to my brother or sister in his or her anguish, that opens me up to the slow, almost imperceptible process of building trust and friendship. It is this slow process of building relationship that creates the space where healing can happen.

Secondly, there is the professional dimension of competence and expertise. This is a vital component of the healing process in L'Arche. As in the case of Danny, it is necessary and helpful to work with people who have a professional expertise in such areas as neuroleptic medication, secondary handicap and mental health issues, including mental illness, as well as social rights and health legislation. Working within the context of a multi-disciplinary team, comprising L'Arche assistants who have an intimate and subjective knowledge of the person as a result of living and working closely with them, on the one hand, and people from outside the community such as a psychologist, GP and social worker, who bring an objective and specialised perspective, on the other, provides an extremely valuable tool in this process.

Thirdly, there is the spiritual dimension of the healing process. L'Arche's spirituality is based on the particular insight that God is hidden in the most vulnerable and broken people in our community and that he is also hidden in a special way in those parts of my own being that are vulnerable and weak. It is in welcoming the weakness and vulnerability in Edith and Danny, and within myself, as I accompany them on their journey, that together we are led to growth and to healing.

I have discovered through my friendship with Edith and Danny and others, the paradox that they have been a source of healing for me through their unconditional acceptance of me as I am and through their simple trust in me. They have helped me to see that the healing process in L'Arche is a mutual and reciprocal one. It is to the extent that we suffer together, and share the hurts, that we also grow together.

Conflict and Reconciliation: Discovering a Common Humanity

Conflict, and the hurt and anger it gives rise to, is one of those hard, inescapable realities of community and, indeed, of family life. As I already mentioned in the introduction, it occurs at all levels of community life, and no one, from the community leader to the newly arrived house assistant, is immune to it.

I remember during my time in L'Arche Trosly working as part of a leadership team of four house-leaders in the biggest L'Arche house in the community, called Le Val Fleuri. It is not a structure I would recommend. Working as a team of two house-leaders is challenging enough, but four is bordering on the precarious! Jean Vanier was one of the four leaders. He was a wonderful support and presence when he was there, but he was away on the road much of the time giving retreats and visiting communities all around the world. Of the other two house-leaders, one was a big hearted and compassionate Italian by the name of Maria, and the other was an energetic French woman with a wonderful, earthy sense of humour, called Anne. Both of them were highly gifted and capable women with good organisational and leadership skills. The only problem was that they both liked being in charge, and the fact that one was Italian and the other was French didn't help matters.

They couldn't see eye to eye about anything! They were constantly disagreeing with each other, and often their language was colourful in the extreme. *'Merde!... Salaud!....Espèce de con!'* I remember thinking how much nicer bad language sounded in French than in English, as they shouted abuse at each other one day in the kitchen! Fortunately enough, I got on well with them both, but I did sometimes feel like a UN peacekeeper in a tense multi-ethnic conclave. This, don't forget, was the leadership team! The experience certainly helped me to develop my conflict-resolution skills, but in a way I had not quite anticipated.

It was a good preparation for my time as director of the L'Arche community in Cork, where I was often called upon to facilitate reconciliation and conflict resolution between different members of the community, be it a misunderstanding or a row between two core members, between a core member and an assistant, or indeed between an assistant and a house-leader. Sometimes the conflict was between one of the other leaders in the community and myself!

Living at such close quarters, as in a family, it is inevitable that we are going to rub off against each other. This is compounded by the fact that we are all so different, coming from different cultures (my house in Trosly that year, which I led with Maria, Anne and

Jean, comprised eight different nationalities, four of them in the leadership team), social backgrounds and religious denominations, not to mention the differences of gender, age and intellectual ability. I would often say to newly arrived assistants during my years as community leader that what is important is not so much that we sometimes have fights or disagreements in our life in community, since they are an intrinsic part of our life together. What is important is how we respond to these conflicts, and take responsibility for them.

I have been touched by the forgiveness shown to me by different people in my community, and by hearing those most graced words of release that anyone can give you: 'I forgive you'. Receiving those words in different ways from Danny and from other core members and assistants in my community, has been a powerful and humbling experience for me. One of my greatest joys as community leader was to witness, often as a third-party facilitator, such moments of reconciliation between brothers and sisters who had become 'enemies' in community.

Seeing them having the courage to name the hurt, exchange in their own way those graced words, 'I'm sorry' and 'I forgive you', and extend the hand of friendship as a gesture of reconciliation, has been an inspiration to me. This is not to say that the process of reconciliation ends here, with these words and gestures. Reconciliation is a complex process and time is needed for healing and integration. These experiences have, however, convinced me of the extent to which forgiveness is a healing and transforming experience.

It is through experiencing such moments of conflict, and working through them in a spirit of reconciliation, that we truly build community and a sense of belonging. We discover, in that process, our common humanity. Behind our roles, and the masks we often wear, we are all vulnerable and struggling human beings whose hearts are more needy than we would dare to admit at times.

On the inside, we are all sensitive and easily hurt. We are also capable of hurting others. Fundamentally, we all carry the same yearning to love and to be loved, to be valued and appreciated for who we are as individuals, in our originality and uniqueness.

My life in community has taught me that what unites Danny and I, in terms of our shared humanity, is deeper and stronger than that which divides us. Whether we are intellectually disabled or supposedly 'normal' (whatever that means), whether we are young or old, from the north side or the south side of Cork city, French or Italian or Irish, we share a common humanity. In this we also share a fundamental equality as brothers and sisters belonging to the same human family. We discover that we need each other, that we are inter-dependent. As Danny would say, 'we're brothers, you and me! We are all brothers and sisters'. Here is an inclusive vision of humanity, which opens us up to the notion of difference as something to be valued and celebrated, rather than as something to be feared and rejected. So often the one who is 'different', 'the stranger', in our society is excluded and treated with prejudice and contempt. People like Danny invite us to not be afraid of them, but to listen to their story and to become their friends.

Busyness and Spirituality

In L'Arche, busyness and spirituality go hand in glove. Much as I often wish it were otherwise, this is the reality! I remember my first year as a house assistant in L'Arche in Trosly as an experience of slowing down and becoming more friendly with time. I had come from a busy life as an academic.

I had always had at least three major projects that I was pursuing at the same time! Coming to live with Edith and Loic and Yvan in La Forestière, a house for ten people with profound disabilities, who needed total care in terms of the simple necessities of life, such as eating, bathing, dressing and toileting, was an experience that obliged me to slow down radically my pace of life. As I struggled awkwardly to give Yvan and Loic their bath each day, to dress them and to feed them and to get to know their ways, I began to realise that I was no longer living quite so much in my head but was being called by my friends with learning disabilities to draw closer to my heart and to my body. They called me to live more at their pace and rhythm, which was a slower and more gentle one.

At the same time I was struck by the contrast between the relaxed pace of life of the core members in my house and the busy and stressful pace of life of many of the assistants, especially the house-leaders. I was not surprised when I saw all they had to do. Running a house for twenty-two people (including assistants), caring for the complex and demanding needs of ten people with profound learning disabilities, organising prayer times, helping to organise community events and celebrations, all on top of living the intensity of those relationships in the house for almost twenty-four hours a day! The dual identity of L'Arche as faith community and service provider for people with learning disabilities does indeed create a daunting workload and an intensity of life. While it enables the core members to enjoy a relaxed pace of life, it often calls the assistants to assume a more busy and demanding rhythm.

Nonetheless, I discovered during that first year in Trosly how certain of these assistants and, also, other long-term assistants in the community whom I had got to know, radiated through their work a quality of deep contentment and joy. Though they were very busy and active people, they never gave me the impression of being in a rush or not having time. In fact, they would nearly always have time to stop and say hello to me and ask me how I was doing. They gave me the distinct impression of being very free human beings, very much alive and at peace with themselves. They helped me to realise, more through their actions than their words, that it is possible to integrate a very busy and active life (which is both person- and task-orientated), with a vibrant and living spirituality. They showed me that not only is this possible, but it is necessary, if one is to live the busyness well and in a life-giving way. They revealed to me that Martha and Mary, action and contemplation, are not enemies, but sisters and friends, and that both are an integral part of the spirituality of L'Arche.

As I look back on my own spiritual journey in L'Arche over the past seventeen years since that first year as an assistant in La Forestière, I realise that I have indeed been nourished and sustained by this spirituality, in the midst of the busyness of my life in community.

Firstly, I have been shaped by an aspect of the spirituality of L'Arche, which Jean Vanier calls 'the way of the heart'. When Vanier speaks of 'the heart', he is not referring to vaguely defined emotions, or still less, anything that touches on sentimentality; rather he is speaking of 'the very core of our being', that which is 'deepest in each of us'. The way of the heart puts people first, and is the spirituality of what the Jewish philosopher, Martin Buber, calls 'I-Thou' relationships, where one human being is present to another in a relationship of communion, person to person, in the present moment. Not a relationship of 'I-IT', as a subject relates to an object, but as subject to subject, person to person. God is present in such relationships of communion between human beings, Buber asserts (Martin Buber, *I and Thou*).

As in other areas of life in community, here again I have discovered that my brothers and sisters with learning disabilities are my teachers and guides. During my latter years as director of the L'Arche community in Cork, when I was often very busy and stressed by the administration, planning and 'problem solving' side of my role, Rita would come and say to me: 'I'm getting worried about you Tim. You're very busy and I haven't seen you for ages! Can I meet you for lunch and a chat sometime?'

She was calling me back to my friendship with her, which was, and still is, important and nourishing for us both. She was telling me not to forget, in my busyness, the way of the heart. In other ways, and at other times, Rita, Joe, Nuala, Veda, Danny and others have led me from my own serious, busy and cerebral world into a world of celebration, friendship and laughter. They have saved me from myself on numerous occasions, and have been for me a prophetic voice calling me back to the essential meaning of my life. That is perhaps why the Charter of L'Arche gives an important place to our core members as being in some way the guardians of our spirituality:

> L'Arche communities are communities of faith, rooted in prayer and trust in God. They seek to be guided by God and by their weakest members, through whom God's presence is

revealed. Each community member is encouraged to discover and deepen his or her spiritual life and live it according to his or her faith and tradition. Those who have no religious affiliation are also welcomed and respected in their freedom of conscience.

The beauty of it is that our 'core members' live their spirituality in a totally unselfconscious way, by simply being themselves, and by living in the present moment. Whether an assistant belongs to a faith tradition or is a committed atheist, makes no difference to them, as long as the person is willing to be their friend.

Secondly, I have discovered in L'Arche the need to take time each day for contemplation and prayer if I want to be faithful to my vocation of friendship with Jesus and to grow in the way of the heart. As the poet T. S. Eliot puts it: 'at the still point of the turning world, that's where the dance is'. I am fortunate in my L'Arche community that time for prayer and reflection is part of the structure of each day, and I find these moments of prayer in community both nourishing and bonding.

However, time for personal reflection and prayer each day, where I can go to my room, light my candle and sit in my prayer corner, is equally important for me. Time where I can get in touch with the mystery of that secret place within me where God dwells and where love is present.

These times of daily prayer, both personal and communal, more than anything else, free up the creative energies of love in my heart, and enable me to be present each day to my life in community and to find in it a deep contentment and joy. In my moments of darkness and of doubt, they help to keep alive in me the seeds of trust, and of hope. As Brother Roger of Taizé puts it: 'Trust and hope are rooted in a mysterious presence, the presence of Christ. Since his resurrection, Christ has been living in each of us by the Holy Spirit'; still more, he is 'united to every human being without exception'.

Thirdly, my family (my wife Maria and our children) has been an integral and sustaining part of my spiritual journey in L'Arche over the past twelve years. Maria and I have discovered that we can live an authentic vocation in L'Arche and in the Church today as a married couple and that we do not have to be a priest or a nun to do so. Our vocation as a couple to live 'the way of the heart' has been, and continues to be, a source of blessing, of challenge, and of great fulfilment for us both, and for our children. L'Arche, as a vocation, calls us to endeavour to centre our life on God, and on 'the little ones' in our life, that is to say, our own children and our brothers and sisters with learning disabilities. While it has called us as a couple to service, and has stretched our resources to the limits on occasion, it has also greatly enriched our life as a family, in many ways, both humanly and spiritually.

In order to last the pace of 'the long walk' of my vocation in L'Arche, I have discovered that I need to take responsibility for my own personal and individual journey. L'Arche cannot, and should not, do this for me, though it can offer support to me in this. I need to be vigilant, to strike a healthy balance between my 'sense of belonging' to L'Arche as an organisation on the one hand, and my sense of individual growth and creativity on the other. There is a danger for me in my life in L'Arche of putting the needs of 'the community' first to the point of neglecting my own needs and compromising the creativity of my own individual journey. Again, I find Martin Buber's insight useful when he describes the two defining instincts of the human being as 'the instinct for communion' on the one hand, and 'the instinct for creativity' on the other. Both these fundamental needs which pertain to our human nature – the need for loving relationship and the need for creative self-expression and being true to ourselves – are important and both need to be given attention and to be honoured. As an organisation L'Arche has become more aware of this need for balance between the journey of the community and the journey of the individual, if it is to be a place that fosters personal growth and an authentic and responsible spirituality. The danger is in going to extremes, be it sacrificing one's individuality at the altar of belonging and service, or fostering or promoting a culture of self at the expense of the well-being of the community.

Conclusion

In conclusion, let me say that L'Arche is no Utopia. It is a very real place where flesh and blood human beings struggle to live and work together in the midst of much busyness, conflict and pain. It is not an easy life choice and, personally, I am often weighed down by a feeling of hopelessness in the face of the challenge it presents. It sometimes feels like I am trying to live the impossible. When I consider the fragility of so many of our communities throughout the world, and when I reflect upon the reality of our demanding and busy pace of life – the pain and conflict that does not go away, the onerous workload resulting from our dual identity as a faith community and a service provider for people with learning disabilities – I think to myself that I must be mad to choose this reality as a way of life!

This is compounded by the insecurity in which we are called to live in L'Arche at different levels, including the fact there is no guarantee of a long-term salary, nor a permanent job. L'Arche is not a religious order with stability of vows and permanence of financial support and tenure, but a lay Christian community that offers a less certain future.

I am often struck by the gap that exists between this sense of hopelessness we can sometimes feel as assistants in carrying the burden of our day-to-day life in community, and the sense of hope we offer to others – our core members and their families, and many people outside of L'Arche. For L'Arche is, I know, a sign of hope for many people, as the parents of my friends with learning disabilities often remind me.

These courageous men and women, the parents of those with learning disabilities, are in turn an inspiration for me. Their love and commitment to their children is impossible to measure, and fills me with a sense of admiration. They are the labourers in the vineyard who have endured the burden and heat of the day in their lifelong dedication to their children, from birth, through childhood and adolescence, to the adult years, when the sense of responsibility does not diminish or go away, even if their adult child is receiving adequate residential care and support services. They are the unacknowledged heroes and heroines in the still unwritten story of people with learning disabilities.

Just as L'Arche is a place of insecurity and struggle, it is also, as we have seen, a place of blessing and of mystery. Even though I can feel discouraged and overwhelmed at times by the burden of it all, I am also immensely comforted and inspired by this life in community, with all its ups and downs. It keeps me in touch with the mystery and calls me, along with my brothers and sisters in community, into an ongoing journey of growth and healing.

It is here, with the help of my brothers and sisters with learning disabilities, that I have discovered the truth of Jesus' words: 'I bless you, Father, Lord of heaven and of earth, for hiding these mysteries from the learned and the clever and revealing them to little ones. Yes, Father, for that is what it pleased you to do' (Mt 11:25, 26). If L'Arche is a place of paradox, that is because, I believe, it is also a place where 'gospel values', the upside-down values of God's kingdom, are lived out. It is a place where the weak really are strong, where the wounded become healers, and where those without knowledge and power are indeed our teachers and guides.

FOR RITA WITH LOVE

You came home from school
on a special bus
full of people
who look like you
and love like you
and you met me
for the first time
and you loved me.
You love everybody
so much it's not safe
to let you out alone.
Eleven years of love
and trust and time for you to learn
that you can't go on living like this.
Unless you are stopped
you will embrace every person you see.
Normal people don't do that.
Some normal people will hurt you
very badly because you do.

Cripples don't look nice
but you embrace them.
You kissed a wino on the bus
and he broke down and cried
and he said 'Nobody has kissed me
for the last thirty years'.
But you did.
You touched my face
with your fingers and said
'I like you'.
The world will never be ready for you.

Your way is right
and the world will
never be ready.

We could learn everything
that we need to know
by watching you
going to your special school
in your special bus
full of people
who look like you
and love like you
and it's not safe
to let you out alone.
If you're not normal
there is very little hope
for the rest of us.

Pat Ingoldsby

Brendan Kelly is a priest of the Diocese of Galway, serving in Lisdoonvarna parish since 1996. A native of Craughwell, County Galway, he was ordained in 1971, and spent twenty-three years teaching in Coláiste Éinde, Galway, and Our Lady's College, Gort. He has been involved with people who have learning disabilities for many years, for example, as chaplain to 'CLM' and Faith and Light groups. In 1995/6 he lived a sabbatical year in the L'Arche community at Cuise-La-Motte in France.

PRIESTHOOD AND HANDICAP – SOME PERSONAL REFLECTIONS

He who welcomes you welcomes me.

Perhaps I should begin with Braerannoch. This is the name of a house in Scotland that I visited in 1979. It is a house of the L'Arche community. A friend who had gone to live there the previous year as an assistant invited me to come and visit. For a number of years prior to this, I had been involved socially with people with mental disability in my spare time. I had also worked in the preparation of people with more profound handicaps for the sacraments, specifically the Eucharist and Confirmation. I had also just come across a book of Jean Vanier's which resonated deeply with me because of the way it spoke of the vocation and gift of people with learning disabilities for our world. At the same time, Seán, a student friend, when I mentioned the invitation to Scotland, said he'd love to visit a L'Arche community too. The upshot was that as soon as holiday time came the two of us were off to Scotland!

We arrived at Braerannoch around tea-time. We drove up the driveway of this rather large and stately house. Out we got and knocked on the door. The door opened and it seems to me now that the whole household of maybe twelve or fourteen people got up from the table and poured out the door to welcome us. Though we were strangers, everybody was delighted to see us. We were ushered in, places were found for us at the table and without question, we were at home, and part of the family, from that first moment.

What was particularly good at Braerannoch was the fact that this total welcome was for me, Brendan, simply as myself, a human being. It had nothing to do with the fact that I had any qualification, achievement, rank, station or uniform, or that I was a priest. We were simply received as *people*. No need to be anything more. That was enough to merit us a great and joyful welcome. 'The person who welcomes you welcomes me, and the person who welcomes me welcomes the One who sent me' Jesus said to his disciples (Lk 9:48). The Psalms tell us that 'the Lord takes delight in his people', and Proverbs that 'His delight is to be with the children of men'. In an experience like the one I have described, the words of the Scriptures come alive. They become real – in and through people who are extremely vulnerable and deeply disabled. There is a joy in the surprise of this for somebody who, all his life, has dealt so much in the word as something written; that the Word of God is alive in our world in people who will never be able to read it – or any other written word.

That welcome in Scotland is only one example of many such experiences of being received with a total openness and wholehearted welcome by people who are categorised as having mental handicaps or disabilities, people who, of their nature, cannot do otherwise. In a fearful and often violent world, this kind of openness can be highly dangerous. But in a society that warns us more and more to be wary of the 'stranger', the counter-sign is necessary. As necessary as the naked and nailed 'figure of fun' on the cross; as necessary and as real a presence as that in the negligible and fragile host, who allows himself be consumed by me in the Eucharist that I might know the fullness of life.

As I now try to articulate my experience with people who have learning difficulties, so many words of the sacred Scriptures come to mind. Experience illuminating the Word of God, and the Word, in its turn, illuminating experience. Only the gospel makes sense of disability, and disability can be a privileged place in which God chooses to bring his good news to life.

It is a vital and necessary thing for me, as a minister of God's word, to study the sacred Scriptures. All the time. But to come to know its author in a more deeply personal way, one needs to meet him too in the flesh. In the welcome, total and natural, of a Cathal or a Marie at the door of Braerannoch, this is taking place, surprising us with a deep joy. Jesus was at pains, literally, to bring home to humanity the fact that God is Father, infinite in mercy, prodigal in love, a God of welcome for all. The great surprise is that people who are too often judged to be useless by the world and therefore unwelcome in it, are the very ones God has chosen to reveal to us his own face.

It is the Heart that Matters

Somewhere at the heart of priesthood is welcome. The priest is a minister of the welcome of God for all. This is true of him as minister of both Word and Sacrament. The priest welcomes the child (or catechumen) at Baptism. He welcomes all God's family at the Eucharist. Reconciliation is about welcoming back. Indeed all the sacraments affirm us as welcomed, as belonging to the Body of Christ, which is the Church, and to God. This is crucial for our humanity. Isn't it true to say, 'I am welcome, I belong; therefore I am!' It is crucial then that the priest experiences himself as welcomed if he is to know his sacramental role in the lives of the people and carry it out in a way that truly illuminates and brings life.

The gift of a man with Down's Syndrome, like Jean-Claude, whom I met some years ago in France, is that he has eyes only for the person, and for that fragile and tentative heart that beats with yearning for communion at the core of every man and woman. At the time, I had hardly a word of French, and was approaching the rather forbidding-looking L'Arche house with a lot of trepidation, fearful because I didn't have the language. But just as I reached the door, it swung open, and this small man with a beaming smile took my hand and led me in. My fears quickly evaporated as he took me under his wing and made me feel entirely at home. No need at all for words. Jean-Claude had no problem with my language disability. It soon dawned on me that we were brothers, this man with whom

I could not speak at all, for we were at ease. Far more than with the men and women who were assistants, talking away in a language I did not understand.

Jean-Claude is at home with the human heart. He naturally cuts through to that essential core of our humanity. So somebody as verbally efficient and educated as I am finds myself liberated back into my humanity. Essentially, like Jean-Claude, I am a human heart, needing tenderness and longing for communion.

Isn't that what Jesus and his Incarnation and God's saving plan are all about? Affirming our humanity and its goodness, calling us into a new reverence for our simple selves, and reminding us that it is the heart that matters, not the external, superficial things (like colour of skin, language, position, possessions, education, etc.). The heart that beats in the deep inside of every man and woman is the same heart, needing only one thing, the nourishment of love. Jesus came so that we might all speak the language Jean-Claude speaks all the time to anybody who comes to his door, the language of love.

So Jesus does ask us to be reborn. But not into something we are not. Reborn into our own humanity. Back to the heart – out of the world of illusion and superficiality. As minister of word and sacrament, the priest stands at the threshold of this rebirthing process and is its servant. This is what people like Cathal and Marie reveal to me. People who are poor, very poor, by any of the usual standards of earthly kingdoms. Not, however, by the standards of God's Kingdom, which are radically other: 'Blessed are the poor in spirit....' (Mt 5:3).

Going to the School of Humility

When I took a sabbatical year and went to live in a L'Arche house as an assistant, the experience was very different to what I had, in my naivety, imagined. For almost twenty-five years I was used to being recognised as 'Father', and treated accordingly. I tended to be at the centre of things, to know what was going on, to be recognised, consulted, etc. What I would never have believed was that I might thus have acquired expectations as to how I would be treated. I continued to see myself as unspoilt and ordinary. I was quickly disabused of this illusion. Only a day or two working intensely at menial tasks like making beds, cleaning toilets, etc., with people half my age, and at sea as to whether I was doing them at all as I should, because I couldn't understand the language, was enough to wake me to the not very palatable fact of how attached I had become to the perks of rank and station. I found myself resentful of the young and what I perceived as their patronising attitude towards their grandfatherly colleague. I hated my own ineptitude in the language, and the aching bones and the straining middle-aged back. And I was angry at what I experienced as the general disregard for me. I, so used to being at the dead centre, found myself uncomfortably at the very margins! A Polish priest said to me once, 'Being without the language is a real school of humility!' It certainly is! Père Thomas Philippe, who founded L'Arche with Jean Vanier, quoting St Bernadette, said, 'One must experience an awful lot of humiliation to gain even a little humility.' Human respect is a dangerous thing. It can lull one into a world of self-delusion. I had to admit I had been badly in need of the very painful humiliation that I was silently and privately experiencing. And in all of that I began to experience myself as very close to the six very disabled people at the heart of our house. And close, as never before, to the Jesus of Golgotha. I began for the first time, after twenty-five years of the daily celebration of Mass, to know in my bones, as it were, a little of what this holy sacrifice is all about. And that holiness is unbearable. So is handicap.

Into the Darkness

The speaker spoke quietly but passionately. Her love for 'people with handicaps' was clear. She had used this word 'handicapped' a few times when Dominick interrupted. 'I don't like that word' he said. Dominick is in his mid-thirties and had lived since very early childhood in institutions, some of which were not good. He cannot read or write. He lives and works in a sheltered situation. The speaker paused and looked at him. She responded gently, 'and how would you say it, Dominick?' His eyes dropped and, very quietly, he said 'I suffer'. That was all.

The late RTÉ journalist, Kevin O'Kelly, in a classic 'Thought for the Day', spoke of the experience of being the parent of a son, Kevin also, who had a serious mental disability. His last words were 'Handicap is hard'.

Unbearable. Suffering. Hard. This is what handicap is. For the person with the handicap. For the parents. For everyone. So there is another side to the story, diametrically opposite to the welcoming, life-giving reality I've been exploring up to now. Disability is a dour and difficult, silent and non-communicative thing. It means floods of bitter tears, anger, violence, disturbed nights, impossible days. It means exhaustion for parents and carers, being at one's wits' end, driven to distraction. It causes family breakdown and depression, and wounds that never heal.

To experience anger in the face of a strong, healthy, 'normal' person is difficult enough. To experience it, and the urge to violence, in oneself in the face of a person one is supposed to be caring for and who is obviously defenceless, is intolerable. Priests, above all, are supposed to be people of compassion, especially with those who are clearly weak and vulnerable. It's how I'd always want to see myself, certainly.

But all of this has been severely tested. By Alan, for example. He is a young man in his late teens. He cannot speak, walk, or do anything at all for himself. His eyes never meet yours. He lives in a world of his own. Because he was relatively small and thin, carrying him was not too difficult. Until he chose not to co-operate. Then he became rigid, dead-weight, very heavy. Too awkward for me to handle. This would often happen in the course of dressing or undressing him, making the task almost impossible. For me at any rate. Then I'd find myself boiling inside. Wanting to shake him, scream at him, or just throw him there! His going on strike, as it were, aroused in me the impulse to strike out at him. But for the shame it would be, anything might have happened. This deeply wounded man who had been abandoned soon after birth, fatherless, motherless, belonging to nobody, ought to have aroused in me the deepest compassion and pity and love… but no. He revealed to me rather a darker self, that part which years of education and respectability had taught me to pack away carefully to the point that

I had almost forgotten it existed. What was particularly nasty and shameful in the eyes of my own carefully constructed self-image was the fact that I could harbour such violent reactions to a young man who had already known far too much violence and brutal abandonment in his life. So there I was, thanks to this man of such deep disability, face to face with my own shame, brokenness and incapacity.

My plan had been to be good to him. To give to him. Instead of that it was he who gave to me – a short, sharp lesson in the truth; the truth about myself. The hard and vulnerable truth; self-righteous, sinful, proud and not so graciously accepting the loss of youth and its powers.

And yet am I not the one who goes every day to the altar of sacrifice to re-enact sacramentally that awful passion and violent death of the most gentle and vulnerable of men, Jesus? Somehow to do this with authenticity demands identification with the victim, but also with the perpetrators of that abusive and violent crucifixion. A crucifixion that continues intensely in the lives of so many people with learning disabilities and, through them, in the lives of their carers.

A Good Shepherd

The celebration of the Mass has to do, first of all, with acknowledging the pain and anguish, the Calvary realities in our lives; and then the transformation of these realities in Jesus, our risen Lord. Because of Alan and his likes, I hope I approach the altar now a little more authentically and less arrogantly. And knowing again, a little more clearly, what I am about.

There are many comforts in being a priest. One's material welfare is well taken care of; there is always a house, a bed, a table. People are extraordinarily caring and affirmative. Even more so, in recent times, in face of all the public questioning and the demands of more 'transparent' times. The temptation to opt for the comfort is always very real. The ones amongst God's people, therefore, who disturb us are a blessing.

The Curé of Ars, in a memorable phrase, said that 'priesthood is the love of the heart of Jesus'. A great gift of people with disabilities is that they open up this whole world of the heart to us – our own hearts and the heart of Jesus. The love of Jesus' heart is, first and foremost, expressed in obedience; that deep listening to, and 'yes' to, the will of the Father – that he be the instrument of his salvation. This is an 'obedience unto death' (Phil 2:8) as St Paul puts it, the ignominious death on the cross. The sacrifice that takes away the sins of the whole world. Obedience unto being reduced to the status of the Lamb of sacrifice – innocent, defenceless, incapable of protecting himself. There are so many in the world of disability just like that! Isn't it with these, still weak, sacrificial victims to the idols of efficiency, strength, and power, that Jesus identified? Precisely because of this identification with the lowly and the defenceless victims, 'God raised him up' to be the great Shepherd (Hb 13:20). Paradoxically, dying he restored life; becoming lamb he became shepherd, 'so that every tongue would proclaim Jesus Christ as Lord' (Phil 2:11).

A priest is an icon of Jesus the Shepherd. As with Jesus, one becomes a true shepherd only insofar as one allows oneself to become the lamb; identified with the victim, the defenceless, the most vulnerable. Not in any notional sense but really and truly. This is where the love of the heart of Jesus leads, to the Bethlehem stable, and to the cross of Calvary.

As Little Children

The prophet Isaiah predicted that in the messianic times, the leader would be 'a little boy' (Is 11:6). 'Unless you become as little children…', Jesus said when ushering in that time, 'you will not enter the Kingdom of heaven' (Mt 18:3). 'It is to such as these [the little children] that the Kingdom of heaven belongs', he says in another place. The most effective way to preach the Word of God is to live it. The essence of priesthood lies in becoming that child so dear to Jesus, the 'little boy' of the prophet Isaiah. It is in the way of powerlessness that the priest, minister of God's word, is called to be leader. It is here that the insight of the Church, calling the priest into celibacy, makes sense. This way of radical innocence is appropriate for one who would become the word of love he is called to proclaim. A love that would be a radical poverty in every sense, identifying, like Jesus, with all who are poor. Identification, especially for me nowadays, with the people about whom I have been speaking. People like Fergal.

Fergal is a happy man, from a good home. I accompanied him once on a retreat of the Faith and Light movement, designed for enabling people with mental disability to grow in faith.

We were asked to explore together the experience of hurt and pain in our lives, with a view towards the upcoming celebration of Reconciliation. Unconsciously, I took the lead and began asking Fergal about any experiences of pain or feeling hurt in his life. Fergal is a man of few words at the best of times. My many questions all yielded the same happy response: 'No!' Then one time after his 'No', he added, 'Are you married, Brendan?' I never even heard him at first, so focused was I on getting him to talk. But when he repeated it again, the penny dropped. *He* was asking *me* a question, and this was a *sharing*.

My answer ought to have been a simple 'no' too, but somehow that wasn't the way I had heard it. Inside of me it rang out: 'Married? *Why not?*' It was as if I'd never considered the question before. And now the whole area was opening up inside of me. Children, companionship, love... the loss, the emptiness. Barren. Fergal's simple question put the cat among the pigeons in no uncertain fashion. Why all this should happen, at that particular moment, I'll never know.

As I talked to him then, I began to discover a brother. Fergal is helpless regarding his handicap, I am helpless too in the face of my own choice. That free choice, made many years ago, left me disabled too. The call of God is not simply into the Promised Land. It is into the wilderness first. That is the Way. At Fergal's question, that wilderness came alive. But because he was there, I was not alone. And all those other people with profound handicaps who can never have progeny, never conceive or play their part in consummating a union, there I am in the midst of them. Brothers and sisters in that poverty which was also chosen by Jesus. Bonded in love, yes, love with Fergal – and all the rest of them – precisely because we cannot marry.

'What can bring us happiness, many say. Let the light of your face shine on us, O Lord!' The light of his face shines very clearly in the love of a spouse, in the ecstasy of intimacy and its fruitfulness. But he is a God of many faces, and the light of his face shines for some of us through our solidarity, in that seeming incapacity that he confers on some and into which he calls others. To be a minister of the word out of this place of real poverty that is celibacy, enables a more universal and inclusive resonance. For our deepest ground of solidarity with each other, as men and women, lies in our incapacities and limitations. We are blessed because poor in Spirit. Not for any other reason.

God's Ways are Not Ours

Our age seems to believe that salvation is in the hands of 'the brightest and the best', particularly in the intellectual sense. The Gospel, however, is not so sure. 'It was to shame the wise that God chose what is foolish by human reckoning', St Paul asserts in Corinthians (1 Cor 1:27). Long before Jesus' time, the Old Testament knew that God's ways are not ours, for it is a long history of God choosing people who were painfully aware of their unsuitability for the task in hand. People like Moses, Jeremiah, Isaiah and David. 'Take no notice of his appearance or his height, for I have rejected him' (1 Sam 16:7) God said, in no uncertain terms, to Samuel when he presumed the strongest of Jesse's sons would be God's chosen one.

The long history of the Church's involvement in caring for people who are marginalised, who don't or can't make it, is not primarily about caring for them. It derives, rather, from the fact that deep in the Christian heart lives the realisation that these are precisely the people whom God has chosen to be his instruments in saving the very ones who are healthy and strong, and resourceful enough to do the caring. The poor are our masters in every sense – our leaders and our teachers. It is they who will save us, not the other way around.

My own initial involvement with people who have mental handicap had to do, very much, with that laudable desire to help them. One feels very good in a helping role! However, all of that changes. Soon the realisation dawns, 'Who is helping whom?' Imperceptibly the ground has shifted, and I find I am the one at the receiving end: of trust and love, and of a deep calling into humanity and humility. The Christ with whom I fell in love as a youth is no notional or spiritual figure. He is alive and real and present, in the very people to whom, I thought, I was bringing him. This is, initially, a humiliation, but eventually a great liberation. What a mystery in which we are caught up! All I can do is give thanks!

COMING HOME

You told me that body and soul come together when
you see the light in the trees.

I know that feeling,
that experience.
The experience of God, 'coming home' within us,
Settling down to that fire that burns within us,
Coming home to the hearth within our hearts.

Sit with the Trinity therefore at the hearth within you.
Look into this flame within you and while away the hours.
Let the Father, Son and Spirit become the Friday night callers,
The every day callers,
The any hour callers.

Look into the flame and look back.
Recall the hours,
The days,
The weeks,
The visits that these Holy guests have made to your hearth,
The gifts they have bestowed upon your heart.
And give thanks for all that was, is and is to come.
For come they surely will,
Again and again,
If in faith you sit and wait.

Anne McKeon

Anne O'Sullivan is Founding Director of L'Arche Dublin, which is now six years old. Anne previously lived and worked in L'Arche in Trosly, France, and in Tacoma, Washington State, USA. Formerly she was a psychologist with the Department of Education, and lecturer in Special Education in St Patrick's College of Education, Drumcondra. Anne, who suffered a spinal cord injury in a car accident in her early twenties and uses a wheelchair, has written and lectured widely on disability-related issues in Ireland and elsewhere.

THE WHITE STONE

To those who are victorious, I will give some hidden
manna, and a white stone, with a new name written on it,
known only to the person who receives it.
(Rev 2, 17)

L'Arche communities are places where assistants and people with learning disabilities live together in community, growing together. The life can be demanding, both for the assistants and the people with learning disabilities. Assistants come for many and varied reasons, few of them knowing the extent to which, in their life in L'Arche, they will be challenged to grow, to examine their motivations, their assumptions about people with learning disabilities, and the subtleties of power and control that can exist in their relationships, which they must understand as they negotiate the role of L'Arche assistant. In a L'Arche community household there can be ten adults living together, of varying ages, backgrounds and abilities. If it is to be a healthy place where all members can grow, a great deal of living and loving, of hurting and healing has to happen. In this article, reflecting on the experience of living with Annette, a person with learning and other disabilities, I touch on some of the ways in which living together in L'Arche was a journey of growth for both of us, and how, as Annette entered the final stage of her journey, the 'white stone' of the scriptural passage from

Revelations was given to me as a powerful symbol of the discovery of the true self and the journey's end.

Annette was a founder member of our community, L'Arche Dublin, which opened its doors in November 1993. Before coming to live in L'Arche at the age of forty-six, she had been living at home. She had a mild learning disability and epilepsy, which caused her much suffering. Although partially paralysed on her right side, Annette could do almost everything for herself in terms of self-care, needing only occasional help with some difficult things. However, she could not have lived alone.

Annette was a gentle person who was incapable of hurting a fly. She had a natural old-world courtesy and a warm gift of welcome, which she extended to all our guests. She had a very special gift of forgiveness – I have never met a person who had such a capacity to forgive the hurts of yesterday. She loved to sing, had a childlike heart and a child's innocent love of bright pretty things, with which she adorned her bedroom, which was a veritable knick-knack shop.

Annette sat in our living room on her first visit and politely asked for a glass of water, which I fetched for her. Next time round I suggested that perhaps, since she could get it for herself, she should make herself at home. From her reaction I got the clear impression, which was subsequently confirmed in living with her in community, that in general Annette did not like to do things for herself. She called herself an 'invalid'. She would sit for a long time dropping hints that she would like a cup of tea, but since it was something she was able to do, we would studiously ignore these hints, until she clearly asked somebody. We would joke that before coming to L'Arche Annette must have had a slave in her life, who danced attendance on her, but that we did not think that was the role of a L'Arche assistant.

Annette's description of herself was that of 'invalid'. No amount of argument would persuade her otherwise and she was determined to remain so. In time, as we came to know her, we discovered that there were many things that she could do, but due to the power of this description and her lack of self-confidence, she did not believe herself capable, or she was afraid to try. The 'invalid' status has many privileges attached to it. The invalid is exempt from the usual chores of life and given many comforts and solaces as compensation for his or her particular suffering. Taking on the invalid role can bring one a certain power, which may not otherwise be available in one's family or community. Like many people with learning disabilities, Annette had learned that she had very little of what the world values, least of all power. But we found that Annette could wield a sort of power over the rest of us by being late for community meals, or, knowing full well that we dare not leave her home alone, by not turning up when everyone else would be in the car, ready for a community outing.

Annette appeared to have learned along the way that she wasn't able to do very much. She had attended a regular school, where she learned to apply the label 'dunce' to herself, a label that she often used to explain her inability to do something; 'I'm such a dunce, a stupid-head, I can't do anything right' were the words with which she would regularly berate herself. Perhaps to try was too risky and dangerous and it was better not to try, not to do anything at all. In fact, if you didn't get out of bed in the morning you didn't have to face the hassle of it; this was one solution. Annette sometimes remained in bed until late afternoon, buried under the bedclothes in a cocoon of anaesthetising sleep, to emerge tousle-headed and extremely grumpy, with an even worse opinion of herself for having done it. 'Learned helplessness' well described Annette's way of going on.

For the rest of us in the community this was difficult to live with. It begged some questions, like what is L'Arche? Is it a hospital or a nursing home or a hotel? The answer is that it is none of these things, but a home where we live together and love and care for each other. Annette seemed to wish to retreat and withdraw from that scenario, unwilling, maybe unable to live with and care for others, unwilling, maybe unable to choose life in the broadest sense. Our emphasis in L'Arche is on 'living together' over assistants 'caring for' the other members, whereas she appeared to be asking us to be her nurse, servant or parent; roles that we were unwilling to play for her.

Being involved with Annette meant power-struggles. We learned that the real problem often lay with ourselves – in truth, we often wanted to control her – that was the temptation. It was very hard not to want that but to let her choose – especially when we didn't like her choice. She taught us a lot about ourselves and our motives. When Annette took five biscuits with her cup of tea, I found I was distressed; it took me some time to see that this was my own 'stuff'. I usually didn't like her choice, and would suggest other possible choices. I found it difficult to sit and watch her eating the five biscuits – every morning at 11 a.m. and every afternoon at 4 p.m. In time we simply stopped buying biscuits!

What Annette taught us was something about the reality that we cannot change another person – only they can change themselves. No matter how much I disliked it, Annette would make free choices only when she was ready.

Annette had learned to be helpless through years of being controlled by other people and through living the assigned role of 'invalid'. We weren't helping matters if we continued to control her. Enabling Annette to become her true self involved a slow giving back to her of charge of her life and her choices. She didn't want it really – it was a long painful process. Even after five years she would still say to me 'can I have your permission' when she felt like having a biscuit.

I learned that Annette's behaviour was not Annette. She was someone whose behaviour and choices I found difficult to like, but I learned the truism that it is possible to love a person whose way of going on you find difficult. There were the occasions when a lighter, joyful Annette peeped out – in the little kitchen of our first home when we would dance and sing together while doing the dishes; there were the times when we would play a game of bingo together and the peace that comes of being together as companions and friends was between us. Those moments allowed me to see that Annette was bound by behaviour and thought patterns which made her unfree, that somewhere she had learned a script, which she lived, a script that told her she was of little value and no good at anything. Her true self was imprisoned. I learned over time to see that it was not her true self who resisted and made life difficult for herself and us. I longed for her liberation, but knew that only Annette could do that – all I could do was provide the clues, the aids along the way and the faith in her ability to grow.

I cannot say when or how Annette started to choose differently. Annette's behaviour drove me 'bananas' in those first few years. She pushed all my buttons – I who had invested so much in my own independence found myself threatened by her heavy investment in dependence; I who hated the word 'invalid', having struggled and won against my deepest fears of being consigned to that status; I, being more of a night person, who hates getting up early in the morning but does it anyway, found myself in front of someone who just didn't do it. Of course her behaviour drove me 'bananas'. But it also taught me to confront my own baggage, to excavate some of the material in my own depths that caused me to be unfree. Over time it was clear to me that Annette and I were very alike – except that she, in her innocence and transparency, was unable to hide her faults, whilst I kept mine well hidden, even from myself.

In living with Annette, we in the community learned a lot about power and about human growth. Because of her transparency, we were very aware of the areas in Annette's life where she 'needed to grow'. The temptation was to think that we had power to make that happen. On the one hand, it takes wisdom and restraint and some self-knowledge to figure out whose needs are being met when we 'do for' our community members with learning disabilities, rather than taking time and having patience to find ways of enabling them to 'do for' themselves, even if they risk failure. We need to understand the relationship of power that can find us meeting our own 'need to be needed' by 'doing for' rather than enabling them to 'do for' themselves. On the other hand, it also takes wisdom to know that the other's power to grow is not something in our gift to give, but only something that she must find for herself.

It was a difficult process, this taking back of control, this shedding of the baggage that Annette had brought with her, which made her unfree. She was a truly burdened person. On asking her 'How are you?', the inevitable response would be a list of complaints and difficulties. It was a cause for celebration when, on one occasion after being away from the community, I asked this question, steeling myself for the inevitable response, and instead, heard her say, 'Not too bad, thank you!' In four and a half years of living together, I had never before heard this – it was a sign of how things were changing for her. It became obvious that in many other ways too Annette was gaining in freedom; she was becoming more peaceful, more cheerful and was choosing for herself, for example, eating more healthily, taking more exercise. A slow change came about – it was very beautiful. In her first years with us my mental picture of Annette is of a heavy, depressed, sometimes passively angry presence, who would scarcely respond when spoken to, who would not verbally complain when you asked her to help, but would sigh and give an array of non-verbal signals indicating that she didn't like it. The picture that I have from the last year or so is of a light, peaceful presence in our sitting room – Annette quietly knitting, humming to herself and smiling warmly when I entered the room.

Annette died in November of 1998. She had a sudden heart attack at her Day Activity Centre on a Friday afternoon. She was rushed, unconscious, to hospital, where she died thirty-six hours later, without regaining consciousness. Four of us, and her family, were with her when she died in the early hours of Sunday morning.

I was on my way to a L'Arche retreat in Belgium when Annette got her heart attack. On the plane I was reading *The Hungry Spirit* by Charles Handy, where he quotes the passage from Revelations 2:17: 'To those who prove victorious, I will give some hidden manna and a white stone, with a new name written on it, known only to the person who receives it'. He sees the white stone as representing the true self and, as a reminder, always keeps a white stone on his desk. On the evening of arrival at the retreat, I had got the bad news of Annette's heart attack and knew that her death would be very soon. I knew I would be leaving the next day, but joined the retreat for the remaining time. In the introduction to the retreat, each of the retreatants was invited to come up and take a stone from a basket (I cannot remember why); as I returned to my place I realised that I had received a white stone, the very thing I had been reading about in the plane.

In the next few days the symbol of the white stone became very powerful and consoling for me, as I mourned Annette's death and contemplated the meaning of her time with us. The last five years of her life, spent with us in L'Arche, were surely a journey towards greater peace and freedom for her, in which she had begun to be free to love in a new way, to be free to be her true gentle self. It became clear over the next few days that Annette had gone to receive her white stone, with her own special name on it, known only to her and to God. We had had some part to play in helping her along the road to receiving it. It was her final gift to us, this symbol of the white stone, enabling us to see that our journey, like hers, is a journey towards greater freedom, towards discovering our own true selves and, some day, receiving our own white stone.

MEMORY

If I tell you of my pain
Can you stay
Will you turn away?

If I spell out my grief
Can you cope
Or, like a thief

Will you steal away
My hope
Of being heard?

Still she stands at the open fire
Hands soft and wrinkled
Skirt sprinkled with tiny flowers.
My face enfolded as she rocks me to and fro
Ochoneo go deo, go deo
Movourneen o; do dílis ó!

If I pour the poison of my pain
Can you refrain
From saying, 'You'll be okay
I've got lots to do today?'

If you cannot stay or cope or care
I understand
Only please don't hold my hand
And pretend.

I'd like to find a friend
Who still stay
Until I get it off my chest.
The trauma of the past.

This pain, and grief and woe.
Ochoneo go deo, go deo
Movourneen o; go dílis ó!

Anne Kelly

Stanislaus Kennedy, widely known as Sister Stan, is a native of Lispole, County Kerry. She joined the Sisters of Charity in 1958, and has been instrumental in developing and implementing social service programmes that have benefitted thousands of needy people, particularly those who are out-of-home. Sr Stan founded Focus Ireland in 1985 and is now president of that organisation, which helps people to find, create and keep a home. She is also on the board of Combat Poverty and is a member of the Council of State. She lives with other members of her congregation in inner-city Dublin as part of the Stanhope Green community of people who have either experienced or been at risk of homelessness.

HOMELESSNESS OF THE SOUL

In the sixties and seventies, I worked in Kilkenny with Bishop Peter Birch. Bishop Birch was setting out to build a domestic Church with the poor and the marginalised at its centre, which saw everyone as gift and saw bishop and clergy as servants of the people of God. For me, as for most people, this was a new idea of Church, and I was very drawn to this vision and this work. From Bishop Birch I learnt a great deal about what people who are rejected by society can bring us, the gift they can offer us and the beauty they can reveal to us, if we can only stop and look, see and receive.

In the mid-1970s, while I was in Kilkenny, Jean Vanier directed us in a retreat, and ever since then I have visited his L'Arche community, in Trosly in France, almost every year and I have become involved with L'Arche communities in Ireland, in particular helping to establish the first L'Arche community here, in Kilmoganny, Co Kilkenny.

Through all this, Jean Vanier has been a spiritual guide to me and a source of inspiration. Through him, and through my involvement with L'Arche, I have deepened my understanding of what I had already begun to learn in Kilkenny about the beauty of those who are neglected by society. I have learned how the poor can be a source of life and healing to me every day of my life.

As I walk with the poor, I have begun to understand better Jesus' relationship with the poor of his time. He didn't say, 'Blessed are those who are getting on in life', or 'Blessed are those who get things done', or 'Blessed are those who understand'. He said, 'Blessed are the poor in spirit', and his whole life demonstrates his love for the poor and his belief that the poor in spirit and the poor who were rejected by society are blessed. Yes, that is what he meant. He meant that the truculent, the slow, the ones who don't turn up, the ones who mess up things, the ones who cause trouble, the ones who interrupt and make a fuss are blessed. The poor are blessed, the ones we like and the ones we don't like, too.

In the story of the cure of the blind beggar, Bartimaeus, we see Jesus putting that principle into action, as he stops to attend to the man's needs. With no ambiguity, very gently, he beckoned the man to come. He was in touch in the deepest way with this blind beggar when he said, 'What do you want me to do for you?'
When we encounter a poor person, outside the church, maybe, or on the street, we may feel awkward or ill at ease. But if we want to be in solidarity with the poor, we need to learn to be with them, to look them in the eye, to treat them as friends. And they know if we are with them.

I have begun to see, too, that if I feel a distance from the poor, maybe it is because I have my own agenda. Maybe I am not able to be with people who are poor, but am always looking instead to see what I can do. Most of us were brought up that way, always wanting to be doing things, looking for success, looking for control, wanting to know the right people. It is a daily struggle for each of us to unlearn those values and to recondition ourselves. Of course, some people are gifted by God to be great doers, but it is a life-long struggle to learn that the ability to achieve and to organise are not the only gifts we are given by God. We can learn this from the poor, because they are not interested in competition, they are not interested in who people know; this does not impress them.

The poor challenge me to pray daily to discover my true self, to discover more and more the common humanity we all share. They challenge me to go on this very painful journey, questioning my values, striving to be my true self. It is a painful, confusing process.

We are all afraid of losing our identity, an identity that we have worked to achieve.

It is very hard to learn the lessons of the poor if your gifts are constantly being rewarded, when your ability to do, to organise, to achieve is being approved and applauded. The poor constantly challenge me to accept who I am – not what I can do, not what I possess, not what I have done. The poor challenge me to live more simply. A central question for me and for all Christians today is whether we are open enough to allow the poor to change us, or do we want to change them.

The poor, like Bartimaeus, have a lot to teach us about detachment and fearlessness. He stood up, dropped everything, ran to Jesus. He didn't stop to ask, 'What will people think of me? What will happen to me? What will be asked of me?' He didn't have the baggage that the rest of us carry and that can get in our way when we meet Jesus, or when we meet the poor.

As I walk with Jesus and the poor, I realise how lacking I am in faith and trust, how slow I am to believe in the unconditional love of God and how slow I am to believe in miracles. The poor, like Bartimaeus, are full of faith and trust. When Jesus said, 'What do you want me to do for you?' the blind man said, 'I want to see again.' He hadn't the slightest doubt or the slightest hesitation. This was his deepest desire. I find the same with the poor people I meet. They come to me and they are quite clear: 'I want a house', 'I want respect', 'I want a job', 'I want a life for my children', 'I want peace of mind', I want to feel wanted', 'I want to feel I belong'. They have no doubts about what is their deepest desire. Like Bartimaeus, they are ready for the miracle, they are ready to be utterly transformed.

Our deepest desire as human beings is to know that we are loved, that we are loved absolutely and totally and unconditionally. Through this awareness we, too, will be able to love unconditionally, to go out to others and make sacrifices for others. Jesus is waiting to give us this gift of love, the gift of our true selves, who are made in the image of God.

As I walk with Jesus and the poor I have come to see in a new way that my weakness is my strength. Some years ago, I became very ill, but I neglected my illness. I was the director of a big, busy organisation, and at the same time I was trying to help my family to care for my eighty-nine-year-old father. I found it extremely difficult to accept that I had to stop, that I had to take rest, that I was not going to be the person who was in charge of everything. But I became more and more ill, until finally I had to give in. I felt that I was on the edge, afraid to look to the right or to the left, lest I fell into the dark abyss beneath and around me. I felt a sense of helplessness and powerlessness that I had never known before. It was a dark, dark, Good Friday experience.

It seemed to last forever, but in fact it only lasted five or six weeks. Today I can say that it was one of the most important times in my life. A way was opened in me to a new understanding and a new sensitivity and a new hope that made space for my own fragility and the fragility of the most forlorn and the most broken of human beings. As I got well, I began to understand my own humanity. My illness helped me to connect my frailty and brokenness with the brokenness of the world in a totally new way.

From my own poverty and weakness I have learned that no matter how oppressed we may be, we always retain some capacity to choose light over darkness. We can choose to risk ourselves to goodness or to give in to the power that oppresses us. The choice is up to us. When we take risks, when we let the props go and give ourselves up to the struggle, our gifts and potential are more radiant than at other times.

As I walk with Jesus and the poor I have been taught the importance of non-violence and the importance of facing my own violence. It is only when we confront the conflict, the violence and the anger in ourselves that we can truly know ourselves, and it is only when we truly know ourselves that we can be truly at peace with ourselves. We can only become peace-filled people if we first acknowledge our own propensity to violence and conflict and learn from it.

When I was younger, I was a victim of my own anger and self-righteousness. It was only when I took time to examine what was happening in my own heart and how much my resolve to 'put things right' was driving me on, that I began to see how much unrest I had within myself. My inner life, I realised, was a microcosm of the world, being fuelled by anger and self-righteousness.

This does not mean that I am not still angry at times. Of course I feel angry when I think about the fact that two billion people in the world today do not have safe drinking water; when I think how hundreds of millions of the world's people are hungry; when I realise that in every city in the world there are children being bought, sold, prostituted, abused, rejected, neglected and made homeless; when I allow myself to remember that in any night in Dublin, the capital of my own country, in the midst of wealth and economic prosperity, there are children homeless and on the streets. Injustices like these make me angry, but I realise now that it is how I deal with that anger, and continue to work for peace and justice, that is important.

Behind all our conflicts, our differences, our disagreements, ugly and brutal and violent though they often are, we have to hold on to the idea that we are all human; even with deep differences, we are all God's children, and that means we are all essentially one.

After spending nearly twenty years living and working with the social services in Kilkenny, I came, with a heavy heart, to live in Dublin in the early eighties. I did not feel at home in Dublin and I missed my work and my friends in Kilkenny. But very soon I was drawn into a study of homeless women in Dublin, which turned out to be a turning point in my life. That study and that first group of homeless women led me into a whole new area of work, the area in which I have spent my life since then, working with and for people who have no homes, in Dublin and around the country. These men and women, young people and children, have taught me many things and gifted me in many ways.

Perhaps their greatest gift to me was to reveal to me my own homelessness, my own poverty, my own human fragility and my deep desire to be at home with myself, with other people and with God.

As I walk with Jesus and the poor I have been given a clearer meaning of home and homelessness. We have all experienced times when we are not at home within ourselves. To be out of home in our

heart at this level is to be a stranger to love. We are all homeless in
our heart when we feel rejected, when we feel we are not known and
not loved, not precious, when our image of ourselves is poor. There
is something within every human spirit that does not relish that land
of homelessness, yet too much companionship and security covers
over the rawness of reality and prevents us from encountering the
mystery of our inner homelessness. Our homelessness is a secret
territory in which we can discover our true selves.

We have all had moments of desolation, when we have been full
of opposition to everything, when everything that gives joy to other
people seems to delude and deceive us. When we pay attention to
homeless people, we will see people like ourselves who are trying to
form sentences, who are trying to find a way of coping with the
madding crowd, with the terrible noise, with the stress of insecurity.
The homeless person can awaken in us an awareness of our own
homelessness, our own brokenness, our own need for silence, our
own poverty, when the silence of the night tells us about our human
condition. In each homeless person we can find parts of ourselves –
a childhood that has been lost, for example.

In our homelessness of the soul, we can hear the voice of God
inviting us 'to make your home in me', and it is that invitation, that
promise and hope that makes our homelessness tolerable. We can
endure it because we know that, ultimately, we have a home, a home
that will be revealed to us; but in order to reach that ultimate home,
we need first to realise, to recognise and to experience our spiritual
homelessness and to acknowledge and embrace it.

As I walk with Jesus and the poor I have learned the deeper
meaning of community. Recently, I began to live with two other
sisters as part of the community of Focus Ireland at Stanhope Green
in the inner city of Dublin. Stanhope Green is, at one level, a
housing development, providing living accommodation for people
who would otherwise be homeless.

At another level, we are a community of people with a wide
range of potentials and needs, people who are sick and well, able
and disabled. We all share a single space and time. We meet,
touch, embrace and learn more about each other daily. We share

a sacred space – a sanctuary and sanctuary garden – where we replenish our minds and hearts and spirits, all the time learning more about the uncertainties, inconsistencies and ambiguities of our lives.

I have learned that for a community to work takes effort. It takes time and it takes commitment. Its growth and evolution depends on the efforts and commitment of each of us. It means accepting each other's oddities, idiosyncrasies and weaknesses and accepting and acknowledging and facing everything that produces friction or conflict amongst us.

I have discovered the importance of silence and solitude. I have learned how to be alone within the community and that my deepest self is born in silence, and the individual wisdom of my innermost being is replenished in silence.

These are the gifts we bring and offer to our community, and these are the gifts we receive in community. Stanhope Green has helped me to begin to resolve that pull between a fast life whizzing past and the desire to slow down and to live each moment more fully.

I have experienced the great challenge of living close to people who are or have been oppressed or marginalised. When I live in Stanhope Green I cannot ignore the pain of our neighbours. The daily reality of inner-city life is present all the time. Young people who are lost and lonely, people without homes, families broken or breaking up, troubled people with innumerable problems – all are part of our daily life. All the time I am being challenged by the loneliness, the pain, the sadness, the poverty, the oppression of the people around me.

Living close to oppression opens us up to a new understanding and a new compassion. Hardness of heart cannot be maintained for long in the midst of such obvious human suffering. I have discovered and I know that it is only when my eyes have been opened and my heart softened by the poor that I am really ready to begin to work with the poor and ready to change the circumstances of their lives.

God identifies with the poor not because they are more noble but because they are more vulnerable. Those of us who are not poor are much less vulnerable. Being close to the poor helps me to remove my heart of stone and replace it with a heart of flesh. It helps me to see myself as I really am, to see my intolerance, my impatience, my attachment to security, status and privileges. It shows me my frail human nature. Above all, it forces me to search for the meaning of life and what I am called to be. This is not easy. It is a call to a radical conversion of my heart and mind.

Right through my life my deepest desire has been to become a loving person, living in the unconditional love of God. This desire has always been accompanied by struggle – the struggle of my own human frailty. Daily I have seen and said with Paul, 'the spirit is willing but the flesh is weak'.

In the midst of all this I have found consolation in a deep inner peace, a peace that 'the world cannot give'. I have found consolation too in the many people, among them the poor and marginalised, who have loved, inspired, accepted and challenged me in different ways. Among them, Jean Vanier and L'Arche stand out as a central and powerful source of inspiration and strength, reminding me again and again that my strengths are my weaknesses, my weaknesses are my strengths, and if I abide in Christ I will 'bear much fruit'.

THE GUIDE

(for John)

I was told you talked
Till the age of two,
Then gave it up
As a bad idea.

Good on you, John,
Is all I can say.
Wiser than peers
At two years.

Well said, and well done.
May the road rise to meet you!
We've walked a thousand miles
In silence….

And you held my hand,
'handicapped' man,
when we headed down
Dunmore Cave.

When the guide turned the lights off
Nobody spoke….
And you, who can't speak,
Started to laugh.

This is the darkest
Place in Ireland.
When the lights are turned off
There's nobody there.

You can't see your eyes
And you can't see your finger.
Nobody spoke
And you started to laugh.

Peter Brabazon

Curt Armstrong *is from Georgia, USA. He studied literature and religion at Erskine College, Edinburgh University and Yale University. He lived for four years in the L'Arche community, Le Levain in Compiègne, France. Curt currently lives in Decatur, Georgia with his wife, Anne-Christine, where he teaches high school. They are both members of a Faith and Light community.*

ROOTS

Adolescents are in the process of leaving the earth of the given family. They are looking for a new earth where they can put their roots.
–Jean Vanier

One winter day, I was on my bicycle heading through the woods from Compiègne to the little village of Trosly-Breuil. I had on sandals, shorts and a grey wool sweater; I was twenty-three, and the day was damp and cold.

I was filled with questions. I had recently finished a Bachelor of Arts degree in English. I was living in France, in the midst of 'a year off' in which I had worked a bit and cycled a lot. I was now volunteering at a place called L'Arche, living together in community with men and women with mental handicaps. I was trying to decide where to go, and to understand what my faith meant.

I was, at the time, reading five chapters from the Gospels each morning, trying to penetrate into what Christianity was about. The Jesus on these pages was direct, gentle, demanding, caring. In my world, people were going on from college and interviewing with businesses and buying new cars. In this world in France, the people I lived with were simple, sometimes difficult, often full of joy and laughter. I was fascinated. My parents were professors. I was considering graduate school. I had applied that autumn for studies in literature and religion. 'Blessed are the poor', I read. 'Go on and get a fine education and a good career', I was told on all sides by family and friends. 'Move up, accumulate, be a billboard handsome man', the culture around me was saying. 'I just want you to be happy', my mother would tell me.

And so, here in the woods, I was confused; and I was riding to see a man called Jean Vanier, who had begun this place called L'Arche where I was living. I had written to him a few days earlier, for I knew that he was a man who took his faith seriously. I knew that he had a doctorate in philosophy and that he had taught university for a while. Then he had invited a few men with handicaps from an institute to live with him and this was how L'Arche had begun. I wrote to him that I was fascinated by this idea of 'life with the poor', and that Jesus' talking of the poor being blessed had always struck deep within me. At the same time, I was considering going on to do some graduate work at an ivy-league school, and wondering if the possibility of studying was in fact a form of wealth? What might this have to do with being poor and blessed and following Jesus? I was having trouble making sense of it all.

I was surprised and pleased when, in response to my letter, he called me at my home and invited me to come and see him. I had known religious leaders before, however, and I had a pretty good idea of what he would say. He would say 'Don't take those lines about being poor that Jesus says too literally'.

And then he would go on, I imagined, and ask me why I wanted to study, and give me his blessing for this, and send me on my way. I wondered whether I should have worn long pants, as I knocked on his door.

A tall man with greying hair stooped in the old stone doorway to greet me, and welcomed me warmly. He asked me in English if I wouldn't mind waiting in the kitchen as he would be finished speaking with someone in just a few minutes. It was an old kitchen, with Weetabix and a teapot on the table, and photos of people from L'Arche all around the world and the cards they had made on the walls. It was an old stone country kitchen and strangely comforting, with all those pictures and hand-made crafts giving the sense of a large family. Soon Jean came and invited me into his room to talk.

In the corner was his bed, and some books and papers were on the floor. Closer to the door there was a desk, and on his desk was my letter. He invited me to sit down, and excused the mess of books and papers – 'I find that I can't work if things get too tidy' – and then he brought his chair in front of his desk and sat down facing me. He thanked me for my letter, and then he leaned forward in his chair so that his arms were across his large legs, and he looked at me and began to reflect. I had expected him to ask me questions, and in the kitchen I had once more been working my way through the reasons why I wanted to study and the questions I had. But he didn't ask questions, and, gently, he spoke for several minutes.

I remember something like this: 'I understand your questions well. It becomes, I suppose, a question of an invitation of Jesus. As I think of the story of the rich young man in the Gospel of St Mark, I am struck by the phrase, "Jesus looked at him and loved him". He then goes on to tell him to sell all that he has, give to the poor, and then come and follow him. But, first, Jesus looks at him and loves him. I believe that Jesus almost always begins with a call (and, although he spoke in English, he used the French word here) of *renoncement*. It is a relationship of love. Yet there almost always seems to be a call of *renoncement*. The important thing is not the *renoncement*, but rather the invitation of Jesus'.

It was a long talk, or so it seemed to me, and he must have said much more. I was taken by surprise, and I was trying to take it all in. His words were very powerful; yet it was not the power of words in a book, or of ideas: it was the power that I have come to recognise as words that speak not of an ideal that is 'out there', but that reflect simply from a lived reality. While his words were moving, I was most taken with this man, in his sixties, looking at me, taking the words of the Gospels with great seriousness, yet in a very gentle way. It was something incarnational that struck me, a reality of presence, something of a lived love of God.

I remembered that I had a big decision to make, so I caught myself and asked, 'Do you think that Jesus might be inviting me to study?' 'That, of course, I don't know. If I spoke of *renoncement*, this is not something that we choose for ourselves, for if we do there will be a sort of kickback in a few years. The important thing is to listen and to follow Jesus. There is a priest here in Trosly whom you might want to see. He has more time than I do, and he can help you try to discern this.'

We talked for a while longer. His paradigm was very different from mine, or from that of anyone I knew. It took me many years to begin to understand it. For I was looking for guidance and examining issues, such as suffering, the poor, prayer, profession, etc. I was trying to decide what the 'right thing to do' might be. He, on the other hand, was interested in a relationship of love. He was concerned with presence, with persons, with communion. It wasn't primarily intellectual to him: it was lived. When you live it, the questions disappear. He didn't answer questions: rather, he invited. Listen. Live communion. Give of yourself. Trust. Choose. Be. It was only from this paradigm that what he said made sense, and I believe that he would say that it is only from this paradigm that *anything* makes much sense.

And so I left that room with no answer, and cycled back to Compiègne through the forest. Yet I look at this encounter as pivotal in my life. Little by little, I began to learn to lead a life filled with prayer, silence, trust; little by little, questions began to be replaced with lived experience. It seems strange even to write about such things for, of course, they cannot be captured on paper nor expressed. But I find myself here, this morning, in a little house, with my wife looking over the bookshelf, asking me, 'Have you read the Jean Vanier book *Tout Personne est une Histoire Sacrée?*' I pick it up and begin to read through it, and the familiar words are comforting, challenging, inviting.

How can we know the influence of such meetings? What have I learned from my many subsequent years at L'Arche, from my friends Pierre, Michael, Marie, Guillaume, Johnny, Kent, Christian? Who could measure, what book could explain? It is Thanksgiving weekend here in Georgia, and my heart winds its way back down a familiar forest path, inhabited by faces like those on Jean's kitchen wall. And I am giving thanks for roots.

GENESIS

And did the moon and sun conspire
in a mutual pact of sorrow.

And did a cold darkness
cover the land.

And was the hillside's pathways
astrewn with weeping peoples.

And were those three silhouetted figures
transfigured by light.

And did the valley ring
with steeling silence.

And was silence broken
with a cry of human love.

And was that afternoon's
moon and sun's consummation
as radiant as David's
morning star.

And did one awesome day's
new genesis
regather us?

Eclipse us black sun –
fire-crusted moon
with Christ's redeeming grace.

Possess us dark beauty of light.

Bernard Allon

PART TWO

Jean Vanier is the son of a former Governor General of Canada, Georges Vanier. He is the founder of the L'Arche and Faith and Light communities. In 1964, after years of studying and teaching philosophy and theology, he bought a house in Trosly-Breuil, France, and invited two men with learning disabilities to live with him. He named that home L'Arche, after Noah's ark – both a place of refuge and of new beginnings. L'Arche is now a network of more than one hundred communities in over thirty countries.

He is also co-founder, with Marie Helene Matthieu, of Faith and Light, which started in 1971 and which brings together people with learning disabilities, their parents and friends for regular times of sharing, prayer and celebration. There are now 1,300 Faith and Light communities in seventy-five countries. Vanier is one of today's leading spiritual writers, lecturers and retreat leaders and is author of many books, including Our Journey Home *(Hodder & Stoughton, 1997) and* Becoming Human *(Anansi, 1999).*

POWER TO MAKE HUMAN

An Interview with Jean Vanier, 1980

Tim Kearney: As a person who has spent much of your life working with people who have learning disabilities, to what extent do you feel they are a minority group who are discriminated against in society?

Jean Vanier: Without any doubt my experience in l'Arche and Faith and Light has shown how terribly frightened people are of all that is different, of anything that is alien to us, or with which we are not at ease because of its seeming irrationality. People with a mental handicap are marginalised and seem to strike deep chords of fear in others. Why is this? I think it is probably because they are telling us something about our own irrationality and our own capacity to do strange things.

Tim Kearney: What are the symptoms of this rejection?

Jean Vanier: First of all, the ghetto situations into which we
                often put people with learning disabilities:
                institutions where 300 or 400 live together under
                the care of 'specialised religious'. What I mean by
                'specialised religious' are people who are known, or
                who have vowed their lives, for doing good. This
                implies that in order to live with those who have
                disabilities you need to have specially good and
                specially religious people. In Ireland, you mainly
                took the option of creating ghetto situations with
                religious orders, rather than supporting family and
                integrating people with learning disabilities into
                society. We have experienced similar attitudes in
                our own communities where we have received gifts
                of old, broken television sets! In other words,
                people are prepared to give broken gifts to broken
                people. In France, you find many people with
                learning disabilities in psychiatric hospitals. And
                there is all the pain and disillusionment in the
                hearts of parents when they learn that their
                newborn child has a handicap. The flowering of
                life and activity seems to be denied to people with
                a mental handicap.

Tim Kearney: Inside the institutional context?

Jean Vanier: No, I am thinking of the parents who feel deeply
                distressed because their child has a handicap. A
                whole lot of questions come up in them: Why? Is
                it because we have sinned? And depending on
                the various cultural, religious and social factors,
                elements of guilt rise up in their hearts and this
                sense of guilt is then transposed onto the son or
                daughter.

Tim Kearney: Do you think this may be a paradigm of what happens on a broader social level, in terms of putting people into institutions and so on?

Jean Vanier: So often a handicap is identified with 'evil' and because it is evil we must not look at it. People with disabilities can become a sort of scapegoat. Other people see only their irrationality and their bizarreness and are unable to see the person behind the handicap. You find the same sort of attitude towards people in the prison world. It is as if we need to put people in prison in order for the 'just' to feel justified.

     You find the same reality in every country. In India, for example, in relation to those who used to be called 'untouchables'; in France, in relation to the Algerians or those who are called 'travelling people'. Marginal groups are being pushed into deviant situations in order for the 'elite', at the centre, to prove that they are good, 'the best'.

Tim Kearney: So it's as if there's a pressure in society that cements the relation between those who are strong and at the centre, and those who are despised and at the margin? But do you not feel that those people on the margin of society, those who are despised and misunderstood, can in fact play some sort of positive role in society?

Jean Vanier: One of the greatest difficulties for society and for people is what I would call 'resistance to change'. Some people hide behind their boundaries and their houses with the 'Beware of the Dog' sign up, resisting all change. This is not simply on a physical level, but on the psychological level as well. More deeply there is the attitude of 'I am right, they are wrong – I have the good life'. You find this in all theories of the selection of race. You find it at the basis of all prejudice: 'the blacks are bad', 'the slaves are bad', the ill, the suicidal, the delinquent, etc. But all this is used just to prove that 'I am right'.

What happens, however, when people start to listen to the young woman with a learning disability or to the man in prison or to the newly arrived immigrant? They begin to discover that this woman, that man has a heart and has value, and that maybe their own cultural values are not the only right ones. Then the prophetic cry of those who have been marginalised becomes a cause of change and new life. Because resistance to change is a form of death. People will eventually suffocate themselves inside of their culture, inside of their riches. Whereas those who appear as marginal are crying for openness, calling people to change. They are saying: 'break down your barriers, come out from behind your walls, because behind your walls you are going to die'.

There are many ways in which this call transpires. You have the cry of the revolutionary or of the young person caught up in delinquency, which is a cry for justice and truth. The cry of people with learning disabilities is quite different, closer to the values of the heart. And when you see the Down's Syndrome person, there is a quality of simplicity that can be terribly threatening to somebody who is complex. This simplicity can awaken the heart of individuals who have hidden themselves behind the complexity of their inner and outer barriers.

Tim Kearney: What's interesting about your own particular concern for people with a handicap is that your listening to these people took a concrete expression. It wasn't just a response marked by well-wishing or goodwill, but took concrete form in the communities you established as half-way houses between the institutions on the one hand, and society on the other. Do you think that listening to the people on the margin of society is enough, unless one is willing to listen in a way that will register change in society?

And what importance do you attach to community as a viable way of life, not only for people with disabilities coming out of institutions, but also its wider potential, for prisoners perhaps coming out of the same situation, for all marginal people of society coming together in a community situation? How viable is it, in other words, as a social ideal?

Jean Vanier: I believe that if we start to listen to the person who is weak and in need, our hearts are touched, new energies are born. We are necessarily impelled towards the creation of something new. When we have met people living in an institution, then we become their friend and want to do something. We may want to say 'Come and live with me!' So then it comes down to the practical realisation of living together. And we discover the particular gifts of people with learning disabilities to call people to relationship, to community, to celebration, to rejoicing.

Is this viable for everyone who is marginalised by society? Is it viable for the prisoner? Is it possible for those suffering from a mental illness? Here we are touching on the complex question of the conflict between person and culture. People with learning disabilities are not so influenced by culture; conventions and norms mean very little to them. They are seeking relationship, personal, heart-to-heart relationships. But this is not quite the same for the man or woman who has come out of prison. They may also be in need of relationship but do not want community and all the exigencies of community life, because they have come from a situation of living together that was imposed on them. They need opportunities for a job, to earn their own living and get ahead, etc. For them, the phenomena of culture are far stronger.

So to come to the second question: in point of fact our society is breaking up, through people not knowing what community is about, and possibly through fear of community. Community means commitment one to the other. There is a desire at the moment to get ahead, in a sort of competition and rivalry, which results from the outburst of individualism.

In order to discover the importance of community we have to realise somehow that individualism can lead to death. We may have money, we may have power, but the one thing that is essential is missing – the heart. We realise that happiness doesn't come from exteriority but from interiority. Is it possible to discover this without an experience that makes us realise that what we have been striving for, for so long, is in reality not life-giving? This can come either through an experience of God, a personal encounter with Jesus or an experience of true community, or through a disillusionment with social values. This disillusionment is deeply

present today. Many people who, in the fifties
and sixties, had the optimistic belief that we
would be saved through technology, realise now
that we have technology but are lacking in warm,
faithful human relationships. We may have
power but we don't know how to use it. This is
engendering a deep insecurity, which can in fact
bring people together.

Tim Kearney: So you would say that this current breakdown of
society is a step towards its reconstruction more
along community lines?

Jean Vanier: Right – it can lead to the birth of community.
You see this inside some parishes which have
become more fully alive; people are really coming
together. You see young married couples leaving
their jobs, even though they were making good
money, because they realise it was throwing them
more and more into hyperactivity, destroying
their family life, a life of relationship and
commitment. Without any doubt there is a
swing towards community. We see this also in
the creation of sects, which give a false security to
those who are more fragile. But at the same time
there is this gradual movement towards the birth
of liberating communities, which bring peace.

Tim Kearney: On the question of the relation between
individual morality and positive law, there is a
particular problem in the Irish context. And it is
a problem that has political ramifications because
of the situation in the North. What are your
feelings on the relationship between Church and
State?

Jean Vanier: My own feeling is that it is dangerous for the
                    Church to seek too much help from positive law.
                    Instead of the Church creating dynamic and
                    loving communities and being a place of
                    nourishment, that is to say, a place of nurture for
                    the inner life, it becomes legalistic and eventually
                    tends to support the State. Then you have a very
                    complex situation where the Church becomes
                    more legalistic than life-giving. The early
                    Christians had realised that the laws, the
                    injustices, the perversities of the Roman State
                    were not good. But they had received an inner
                    force, the Holy Spirit, so they didn't need the
                    State to tell them what to do. On the contrary,
                    they realised that what was happening in the
                    State was leading to death, and that through
                    their life in and with Jesus, they were called to
                    become more fully alive and to give life to others.
                    The State, therefore, was in no way a help for
                    them. They had this inner nourishment which
                    came from the fraternity and communion of
                    brothers and sisters among themselves, sharing
                    the body of Christ and giving thanks. This
                    created within them a dynamism and strength.

Tim Kearney: Do you think that they'd have had that
                    dynamism and strength if the Roman Empire
                    had become there and then a Christian Empire
                    and had imposed Christian laws on a State level?

Jean Vanier: Opposition creates a certain dynamism within
                    the minority group, like the Christians during the
                    Roman Empire. Once you have the whole State
                    behind you, however, this inner dynamism is lost.
                    This does not mean that we should not hope that
                    the State would discover and encourage certain

Christian values. But it means that we have to discover active forces within the community in order for it to remain dynamic, even if there is no immediate persecution. I personally feel that there is a great danger when there is too much of a link between Church and State. We are discovering today that the Church must be comprised of dynamic communities of love, that it is not so much the State that is going to change people, but rather the dynamism and love within the Church as a place of nourishment.

Tim Kearney: So you would believe then in the ideal of a pluralist society, where different racial and religious groups are allowed to co-exist without the State law coming out in favour of any single group?

Jean Vanier: It's very difficult to say what the State should be. But what I do know is that each community should become dynamic with love and compassion, and that the State should be respectful of every minority. But there again we must be careful. Now and again I hear people say that abortion is a 'Catholic problem'. Next we may hear that inequality of justice is a 'Catholic' problem. Many Hindus and Muslims are very much against abortion and euthanasia, but that does not make them Hindu or Muslim problems! Can't we work together on certain problems of humanity? Have we lost our sense of humanity and our sense of living in a universe that is our home? I am not against the modern world, but the more we get into the world of cement, technology and electronics, the more we need to learn how to live together as human beings and discover oases of community. I believe that groups of people – and the Church is one of them – should remind us all that to live humanly does not mean that everybody can run around doing whatever they like or killing themselves with overwork; and that if we want peace, certain norms must be respected.

Tim Kearney: Certain norms as 'laws', or certain 'ideals' towards which we must strive?

Jean Vanier: I use the word norm – as opposed to the word law – towards which we must strive, towards which we must orientate ourselves. But what seems to be terribly important, especially for the Church, is to remind people how they can grow humanly. Not to come down as law-givers saying, 'Don't do this and don't do that', but to show that we are called to be and to live something far greater and more beautiful than we dare suspect. We don't have to hide ourselves behind the security of our own riches and cultures. We are called to live something more meaningful. For example, the people in Ireland are not alone; Ireland is part of the world and you can be open to the rest of humanity, to discover your links with the rest of humanity. We must struggle for something that is far greater, much more open, much more divine, much more universal.

The Church should be pointing in a certain direction and showing people that in order to go in that direction, certain norms must be respected. Each person is important and has his or her own point of growth. What concerns me is that morality in the Church has often been focused more on the realm of sexuality than on the realm of possessions. And yet Jesus is always extremely forgiving in the domain of sexuality, but extremely harsh in the domain of possessing without sharing. Jesus never said: 'Woe unto you who are sexually deviant', but he said to the woman taken in adultery: 'Your sins are forgiven, go ahead and love, and love in the right way, because otherwise you are closing yourself off'. But he did say that it is more difficult for a rich person to enter the kingdom of Heaven than it is for a camel to enter through the eye of a needle.

Tim Kearney: Do you think that Christianity as a religion and as a vision of life may, by becoming a religion for the strong, fail to fulfil its full potential? In many countries in the world today there is a sense that the Church has sided with the majority groups in society as opposed to the minority groups, the people on the margin. Do you feel that this is a danger for the Church to which she must be sensitive and alert?

Jean Vanier: The Church has only one guide: Jesus. While on this earth, Jesus lived in a particular way and was close to particular people. As he told us himself, his whole mission was to bring good news to the poor, liberation to the oppressed, sight to the blind, freedom to captives, and to announce a year favourable to the Lord. So it is important that those who are called to render Jesus present – which is the mission of the whole Church – really do render him present in all the fullness of his vision and not some caricature of him. This means being close to those who are poor and rejected and caught up in social, economic and psychological wounds. So frequently we talk of the Church as if it were only the bishops and so on, but it is each one of us, and each one of us is called in some way to be close to those who are weak, marginal, oppressed or depressed. Jesus said that the Kingdom of Heaven was like a Wedding Feast. However those who were invited didn't come because they were so caught up with their own personal projects and the seduction of riches.

It was the poor, the lame, the weak and the blind who heard the call 'Come to the Wedding Feast' and who responded with joy! So the mission of the Church, which is the mission of you and me, is not to condemn, and not to judge, but to *be with* others in their weakness, to *walk with* them in their woundedness, and to be purveyors of hope.

An Interview with Jean Vanier, 1999

Tim Kearney: You have a deep conviction of the ways in which people with learning disabilities can be prophetic. But is this not something of a generalisation? Could you say more about this?

Jean Vanier: I would like to speak in wider terms, about how people with disabilities can change us, open our hearts and call us to new ways of living.

It is like a businessman or a banker who has to be efficient. He works all day long with computers or figures, gives orders or has to make important decisions. When he comes home at night, he can be so tired that he just sits down in front of the television and does not want to be bothered. Or else he can come home to his children, listen to them and talk to them, get down on his hands and knees and play with them. He is a different man! His children call forth something else in him, another part of his being! It is the same way with people who are weak or old or sick or disabled. They call out the child, the tenderness and compassion in us. In that way people with disabilities are prophetic; they have a secret power to change people's hearts and to make us more human.

I remember when I was invited to speak to the theology students at Harvard University. They asked me to talk to them about people with disabilities. I began by reading from the book of Isaiah: 'Who can believe what we have heard? a man of sorrow, familiar with suffering... he had no form or charm to attract us, no beauty to win our hearts ... *and yet it is by his wounds that we are healed...*' (Is 53).

I told them that many of the people I was living with did not know how to read or write or even speak, and yet many of them had a deeper experience of Jesus than they, the students, had. I told them: 'You are looking for a *knowledge* of Jesus whereas people with learning disabilities are seeking a *presence* of Jesus; their intellectual capacity for words and concepts is greatly limited, but their intuition, their sense of presence is greatly increased'.

So, people with disabilities can bring us to what is most essential in Christianity. Christianity is centered on a person, the person of Jesus, the presence of Jesus, who reveals to us that we are loved and who calls us, in turn, to love. There is a double movement: God loves us and calls us to love others; we are called to drink from the source in order to become a source.

Tim Kearney: So what do people with learning disabilities teach us in this sense?

Jean Vanier: They remind us that what is essential is this personal, heart-to-heart relationship with Jesus. I often quote John the Evangelist in his first letter: *'Beloved, let us love one another, because love is from God and whoever loves is born of God and knows God'* (1 Jn 4). In biblical language 'to know' God means 'to have an experience' of God. People with disabilities are teaching us something about the importance of presence and of relationship.

Let me tell you a lovely story that shows this prophetic element of people with learning disabilities. A young boy with a mental handicap was making his First Communion. There was a beautiful liturgy followed by a family celebration.

During the family gathering the uncle turns to the mother and says: 'Wasn't that a beautiful liturgy, the only sad thing is that the little boy understood nothing!' With tears in his eyes, the boy says: 'Don't worry Mummy, Jesus loves me just as I am.'

So there you see the realisation of Paul's words, that 'God has chosen the foolish and the weak to confound the wise and the strong'. The uncle had not really understood. The little boy, in some way, was prophetic.

Tim Kearney: In your life in your community in Trosly, are there any particular people who you would like to cite as having been important for you in that sense?

Jean Vanier: I would mention Raphael Simi and Philippe Seux, the first two men I welcomed in L'Arche. I came from a naval career where I had been taught to be quick and efficient. Then I did several years of intense study and began a doctorate. That implied a great deal of intellectual work. There was something lacking, however, in terms of relationship. I was more a man of action and of teaching. As I began to share my life with Raphael and Philippe and we did things together, I began to change.

Tim Kearney: In what way did they call you to change?

Jean Vanier: They showed me the importance of *being with* others, of entering into relationship, friendship with others, of 'wasting time' together, sharing meals and laughter. They brought out what I would call the 'playfulness' of the child in me.

Through their simplicity, their joking, their need for friendship, they were forming my heart and calling forth tenderness and compassion in me. But they also revealed the anger in me. Because as soon as we start lowering the barriers around our hearts and our defence mechanisms, other feelings can emerge, such as anger or violence. Raphael and Philippe touched and called forth in me what was most beautiful, the capacity to relate, to be sensitive to others and to have fun together, but they also brought me in contact with my capacity to hurt, my difficulties in relationship, and my own inner brokenness.

Tim Kearney: In revealing to you your limits and your shadow side, as you were describing there – your brokenness – was that important for you as a point of growth in your own journey?

Jean Vanier: As I look back in retrospect, I would say yes, but at the moment itself, no. Because it is painful to touch one's anger and violence; it seems to go against our vocation to love and to be close to people, especially those who are weak and poor. A sense of guilt can arise. But this led me to a greater awareness of who I really was. As I gradually discovered my 'shadow side', I realised that I had to work at it and learn how to live through it. Then, what I realised more than anything else was how much I needed Jesus and the Holy Spirit.

Not just psychological help but I needed a power of the Spirit to discover that I did not have to live just from my 'woundedness', but that I could also live from the light that is in me.

At that time, I discovered a letter Carl Jung had written to a Christian woman. Referring to the text in Matthew (25:31-46), he expressed his admiration of Christians who saw a real presence of Jesus in the poor: 'I admire you Christians, because when you see somebody hungry or thirsty, you see Jesus in them. When you visit a prisoner or the sick, when you see someone naked or somebody strange, you see Jesus in them'. Then he goes on, 'What astonishes me, is that you do not see Jesus in your own poverty, hunger and thirst. Don't you realise that you too are imprisoned, in your own fears? Don't you see that you too are sick and that there are strange things inside of you that you don't understand, and that in some way you are naked?'

This text helped me to realise that we all have to work at befriending our shadow side in order to grow.

I also began to realise that one of the greatest fears of human beings is to kill someone in a fit of anger. Perhaps that is why we create walls of prejudice in order to prevent ourselves from harming or killing another person. As I mentioned before, we create walls of prejudice that say 'these people are no good'. Then we don't have to have any contact with them; we can separate ourselves from them and thus the danger of killing them is minimised. I'm beginning to see more and more how prejudices are a part of our protective mechanism, and how they have to be broken down in order to find our source and in order to let what I would call our 'deeper self' emerge.

Tim Kearney: Looking at the Christian Churches in the world
                   today, at the beginning of a new millennium,
                   what, in your view, is their greatest challenge?

Jean Vanier: I sense so much chaos in our world in many
                   different areas: the immense discrepancy between
                   the rich and the poor, the development of
                   armaments and the links between economy and
                   armaments, the developments in genetics, the
                   widespread breakdown of human relationships,
                   just to give a few examples. Then there is the
                   influence of television, which is like a powerful
                   teacher right there in the home. It teaches a lot
                   about violence and sexuality, which a young
                   person usually integrates into his or her life in the
                   context of family. Sexuality and violence touch
                   what I call the chaotic energies within us. So
                   there is something new happening and a whole
                   breakdown of the 'old'.

                       What is the reaction of the Churches
                   confronted with this situation? On the one hand,
                   there is the reaction of: 'we must get together and
                   create strong groups and provide a formative
                   education in order to protect Christian rules and
                   regulations'. This gives birth to strong, rigid,
                   sometimes almost 'sectarian' groups in the
                   Churches. On the other hand, there is a
                   Christianity that is falling into a 'Gallup poll'
                   mentality: if you have enough people saying that
                   something should be done, then that justifies it.
                   There is an absence of any sense of authority
                   except perhaps that Jesus had something to say
                   and that it was important.

                       Yet Jesus himself was at times quite clear and
                   strong in the way he exercised authority. So, we
                   are falling either into an absence of any authority

where everybody feels that they have the truth and can do what they want, or else into protecting ourselves behind the rules of a rather rigid, blind authoritarianism.

My hope is that, just as the Spirit of God hovered over the chaos at the beginning of the creation of the world, so too, as we experience the breakdown of society today, the Spirit of God is there and new life is already emerging within our world and within the Churches. There can be a danger in our Churches of putting structure, morality and dogma before love. But love is our priority. We have to come back to the words of Paul: 'if you have all the languages, if you have faith that can move mountains [which is pretty good!], if you give all your goods to the poor and if you give your body to the flames, but do not have love, then, all that counts for nothing' (1 Cor 13:3).

What is this love? It comes back to heart-to-heart relationships. Relationships that reveal to others their beauty. A love that brings people together, not to a place of intellectual security or power, but to a place of service and unity. As I was saying before, it is often those who are in need who can bring us to this place, to the heart.

Some seminarians, after years of studies, having gone through seminary, and in some cases having obtained a doctorate in canon law, can be so very weak in the area of relationships. They are frightened of relationships, and of the heart, and even frightened of love, because relationships can be linked to sexuality, which causes a deep fear.

One way of helping people to integrate their sexuality, and their hearts, and to become men and women of relationship, is the experience of one-to-one relationship with someone who is weak, elderly, ill or dying. They call forth in us kindness, compassion and tenderness; they can teach us how to listen. They can heal us.

Tim Kearney: So somewhere there is a need for healing?

Jean Vanier: Yes, healing is necessary. In the Middle Ages, there wasn't this terrible breakdown of the family and of society. People were quite structured relationshipwise. What they needed most, at that time, was a formation of the intellect. Today the greatest need is a healing of the affectivity. I'm not saying that intellectual formation is not necessary, it is vital. But there is a more fundamental need of healing because our hearts have been deeply wounded. Healing of the heart takes place through compassion, and the discovery that we are valued and loved, not for what we do, achieve or have, but for *who we are*. That is where Jesus is essentially the healer, saying to each person, *'You are important, you are loved'*.

I often quote the text of Isaiah where God says, *'Do not be afraid because I have liberated you. I've called you by your name and you are mine. If you pass through the waters you will not be overwhelmed, if you pass through fire you will not be burned, because I am the Lord God of Israel, your saviour, and you are precious in my eyes and I love you'* (Is 43). Jesus reveals to each one of us that we are beautiful. As we realise that we are loved and valued by God, we want to respond to this love because love calls forth love.

What I have discovered in my life in L'Arche and through the Gospels is that our most fundamental place of belonging is not to this or that country, culture or religion, but to the human family. Whatever our religion, country or culture, whatever our gifts or limits may be, we are all precious to God.

Tim Kearney: What, in your view, is the core value of Christian spirituality?

Jean Vanier: For a Christian, spirituality is the way we are called to become one with Jesus, and through him, one with the Father and with each other, each one according to his or her gifts and vocation. To become one with Jesus means to see the world, ourselves, other people, especially the weak and the forgotten, as he sees them. To love them as he loves them. This implies a rebirth in the Spirit, a transformation of our hearts of stone into hearts of flesh.

The path on which we are called is given in the eight Beatitudes of Matthew's Gospel, which are the Charter of our lives as followers of Jesus. This means becoming less governed by our own fears, prejudices and our need to be powerful, loved and admired by others, and more governed by the gifts of the Holy Spirit and the presence of Jesus within us.

Tim Kearney: With regard to L'Arche and its dual identity as a service provider (agency) and a faith community, what is the danger, as you see it, for L'Arche today and where, in particular, is L'Arche's point of growth?

Jean Vanier: We have to rediscover a sense of our mission, which is the place and role of people with disabilities in the world and in our Churches. People with learning disabilities are important because what they are crying out for most is relationship. When we begin to listen to a person in need, when we truly enter into a heart-to-heart relationship with someone who has been marginalised because of their handicap, their age, their poverty, etc., then that person begins to discover that he or she is loved and is important. But something changes in us too. Barriers in our own hearts, barriers of competition, of proving that we are the best, start to break down. We discover our common humanity and what humanity is all about. We discover our need for God.

But in order for people with disabilities to grow, they also need good pedagogy. Our communities have to be competent. Things need to be done well. The danger sometimes is to separate too much the agency and the community dimensions. We have to be both a good community and a competent agency.

The agency dimension means that we are attentive to the needs of each person, helping him or her to grow and to become more independent. We have to help each person to be well psychologically. For that, we need good doctors and psychologists. It is important that we do not deny either our humanity or our spiritual life but that we learn to integrate both.

We have to learn to love 'intelligently'. When somebody is depressed or violent, we have to discern what that person needs and how to be present to him or her. It is not just a question of sentimentality or emotions or of holding hands and hugging. We have to find competent help.

To love someone is to bring that person to greater freedom, to help him or her not to be controlled by fear but to become more fully who they are. Then they, in turn, can become a man or woman of compassion.

So we have to come back to a vision of unity in our communities. That unity implies that we have both good psychological help and good pastoral ministers, because human growth implies a wisdom of psychology, of understanding the human being, a good anthropology, but also helping people to grow in love and to be open to the Holy Spirit. If we are unified in ourselves, then we will seek unity around us. Our first call to unity is to bring together people with disabilities and people whose handicaps are less visible, whom society calls 'normal', and to discover that we are brothers and sisters of the human family. But we are also called to work for unity beyond our own community. This means, amongst other things, unity between Christians.

We just have to be attentive to every person in their humanity and come down to the fundamental thing that we must work together for peace, and for a world where there is greater love and greater respect for life and for the human person. So I believe that L'Arche is a call to unity: unity within ourselves, within our community and then between the community and the local church and the local village or neighbourhood and, finally, and importantly, unity with the whole of humanity.

Tim Kearney: In conclusion, who have been the main influences on your spirituality and vision?

Jean Vanier: The first person who really formed my head and
my heart was a Dominican priest, Father
Thomas Philippe. For years I read all that he had
written, I listened to his courses and his homilies
and was guided by him in prayer. The Gospels,
particularly John's Gospel, have influenced me a
great deal. I have spent a lot of time lately with
John's Gospel and, through it, I have
rediscovered the richness of the Old Testament:
the prophets Isaiah, Ezekiel, the Psalms, etc.
Dorothy Day, the Founder of the Catholic
Worker movement in the States, has also had a
great influence on me. And when I started
visiting India, I was deeply influenced by the life
and message of Mahatma Gandhi, his life of
prayer, his closeness to the 'untouchables', his
yearning and striving for unity, the way he called
people to prayer, to the poor and to manual
work, close to the earth.

Later I was touched very much by Oscar
Romero, the bishop from El Salvador, who at the
beginning of his ministry was quite conservative
but who gradually became incredibly close to the
weak and the oppressed, who learned from them
and who allowed them to change his life and his
heart. At other times, Francis of Assisi and
Thérèse of Lisieux also influenced my life. I am
nourished by different people at different times.
But at the present moment the most important
nourishment for me is the Gospel of St John. It is
amazing! Thousands of books have already been
written about it yet you never plumb the depths;
there is always something new to be discovered.

In the field of psychology as well, books are
coming out that are giving a new vision of the
growth and development of the human person

and the quest for love. Many psychiatrists and psychologists are very attentive to what I call the 'positive forces' in a human being. People like Eric Fromm, Alice Miller and Francoise Dolto, just to mention a few. They give great importance to listening to people. By the way you listen to a person and show them that you trust them, this helps them to believe in themselves and then what is most beautiful in them emerges. It is a vision of the human being that is deeper than the will and the reason. It's about the heart, not the heart as an emotional, sentimental reality but as the principle of life in the human being which, if wounded, pushes a person into fear and anguish. If, on the other hand, the heart knows it is loved and respected, it opens the person up to love others. In many writings today, there is a unity between psychology and spirituality.

Ruth Patterson is a Presbyterian minister. She is Director of Restoration Ministries, an interdenominational organisation seeking to promote peace and reconciliation. Her university experience includes Queen's University, Belfast, University of Toronto, Canada, and Edinburgh University, where she did theological training, while applying to be a candidate for the ministry of the Presbyterian Church in Ireland. In 1976 she was the first woman to be ordained in Ireland.

As part of her work in Restoration Ministries she runs courses and seminars on the whole area of healing and reconciliation. These take place in Restoration House, throughout Ireland and in many other countries. Veritas published her first book, A Farther Shore, *in March 2000.*

AN INNER JOURNEY
OF RECONCILIATION

An Interview with Ruth Patterson, 1999

Tim Kearney: This book is exploring the ways in which people with learning disabilities can be prophetic. Do you believe this to be true and, if so, in what ways?

Ruth Patterson: I think that one of the chief ways is that because they are fully themselves, they encourage other people to be fully themselves. With all of themselves that is gift and all of themselves that is brokenness and vulnerability, it's a sort of wholeness that they encourage us to – not just performing, not just an act, but encouraging people to come to the point of saying 'this is me'. Being authentic, and this is the me that God created and loves with all my warts and everything else. But I believe that they are prophetic in other ways as well and the way that

I can best share that is to mention one person who for me has become a very important person. Actually in my room at home I have a prayer board with photographs of people. At the centre of that prayer board is a photograph of Bernard, who lives in the L'Arche community in Trosly. The first time I visited Trosly, I was feeling a bit inadequate and vulnerable and I'd only got school-girl French and I was feeling isolated. I remember on that first day going to the chapel for Mass and I went in and sat down. All these feelings were flooding over me and I was wondering why I'd come. All of a sudden a door opened and this man with Down's Syndrome came in and out of all the places that he could have sat, he came and he sat down beside me.

He took my hand and he started to kiss me on the cheek, and all through the Mass he held my hand and he kissed me on the cheek and I felt so welcomed. Later on that week I was asked if I would like to go on a visit to a Community of the Beatitudes and I said yes. I got onto this little bus and there was only one seat left and that was beside my friend Bernard. All the way there he held my hand and he kissed me, and when we arrived, there was about two hours of worship and he was sitting with me. At one point there was beautiful music and I looked around at his face and never in my life have I seen such a beatific expression. I metaphorically took off my shoes, I felt it was holy ground. I felt that here in this person who cannot speak and who has very little rational thought process, the spirit of God dwells fully, and it was such a moving moment.

When I came back to Ireland, I couldn't
forget Bernard and one day I was away on a sort
of mini-Retreat for myself and I was thinking
about him a lot. I thought, he is a prophetic
voice, a peacemaker, an icon of welcome, of
hospitality, which is what this world needs, so
profoundly and so deeply. So some words came
to me and I found myself writing a poem about
him, and in many places where I go in Ireland
now, I find myself telling people about Bernard
and actually reading the poem. People begin to
weep and I think, 'Lord, Bernard doesn't know
this but he is being used in a powerful way to
communicate that message of welcome and
peace and of hospitality.'

When I was back in Trosly last Easter, I was
at breakfast on Easter Sunday morning and
Bernard came and he started to cry. I said,
'What's wrong with Bernard?' and they said,
'There is nothing wrong with him, he is just so
happy it's Easter'. I could hear him whispering
'Alleluia, Alleluia!' and I hadn't heard him speak
before. And I thought, there it is again, praise
and a closeness to God and a total lack of
inhibition, just being himself.

Tim Kearney: In terms of the mainstream Churches in Ireland
today, how do you see them being called to grow?

Ruth Patterson: Well, I think that the first call is the ministry of
reconciliation. I think that, in a sense, the
Churches are preaching to the converted, and
certainly within the Protestant Churches, again
and again, you hear of people having missions
and evangelising and so on but it always seems
to be to the people who are already converted in

some way because many, many people are leaving the Churches, especially young people. The challenge is to become more relevant and to become more authentic. The only way I know of doing that is a long and slow way.

I think that what needs to happen is that we need to be willing to go on that inner journey of reconciliation, because there is an inner peace process that needs to take place. Unless that takes place, then the outer one won't. But if we are willing to go on that inner journey then that will powerfully affect the outer one. There is no escape from that. If, for example, I'm in a congregation or ministering to a parish, I dare not ask anyone else to do that unless I'm willing to go that way myself. As I seek, however stumblingly, to do that, then there is a sense in which I'm being true to the call of my own life, and that's going to affect other people.

That is what in the end is going to attract other people, not some big flashing lights from the sky, not some big movement, but people who are authentic and who are willing to be open and vulnerable and who are willing to, in a sense, be poor and little and weak so that the strength of God is seen through them. That's what's going to attract and that's what's going to change things.

That doesn't happen overnight. It happens with each person making their commitment before God to go on that journey which is often painful and which will lead us into areas of darkness. I often think of a verse in Isaiah 45 which I love, where God says, 'I will give you the treasures of darkness, riches stored in secret places, so that you will know that I am the Lord, the God of Israel, the one who calls you by name.'

There are so many people who are hungry and weary. They are hungering for meaning and they despair. They need to know the Lord is calling them by name, in other words, telling them that they are special and loved and beautiful in his sight. But if I don't know that for me, how in heaven's name can I communicate that message to others? It's a bit like when the Israelites were crossing the Jordan and Joshua was leading them into the Promised Land. The Priests of God had to go down into the water first, into the cold waters of the Jordan and stand there until everybody had crossed over. So there is a sense in which those people who have in that way committed their lives to working in the Church, through time, have a much greater responsibility to go down there, so that other people can cross over.

Tim Kearney: You were the first ordained woman minister within the Irish Churches. Could you share a little of what this was like for you and also maybe say what, in your view, are the particular gifts that women can bring to Christian ministry and to the role of priesthood or pastoral ministry, in particular?

Ruth Patterson: Yes, I had been working in Queen's University with Ray Davy, the founder of Corrymeela, at the beginning of the Troubles. I began to think that there was a need for some people in Northern Ireland – because of the particular nature of what was happening to us – to be trained not only in theology or only in community work (which was the training I had done in Canada), but to combine both. So I decided to study theology and at the same time apply to be a candidate for ordination, knowing that no Church then accepted women, including my own, the Presbyterian Church. This was the early seventies.

Unknown to me, another girl was also applying but she waited for the Church's decision before she would go and study theology. I went on ahead because to do the theology was important for me whether or not I'd ever be accepted as a candidate. Faced with two applications, the Church had to debate it, and the only reason I was the front runner was because the other candidate waited for the decision and I went ahead to Edinburgh to do theology. It was a very isolated road to travel. It was very hard. I think all of us carry within us things like an inner loneliness, sometimes the fear of rejection and all of these other things, and those were, I suppose, heightened for me on that journey. The whole issue of whether women should be ordained or not in Ireland was being judged, whether I liked it or not, on how one person performed or failed to perform. And that one person was me.

Tim Kearney: How did your colleagues react at the time?

Ruth Patterson: The majority of my colleagues within my own Church stood back and were cautious. Very many were against. So, if it hadn't been for my father, who was also a minister and a dear friend as well, and two or three other colleagues, it would have been totally isolating in that way, in terms of brother ministers. People used to say to me that coming to the point of ordination must have been the most difficult. It wasn't. In Presbyterianism we operate under a system of 'call' or 'invitation'. You have to be invited to be a minister of a parish, and the real test was whether there would be a congregation brave enough to call the first woman.

So I had to wait a little longer than most of my male colleagues but, eventually, I was called to a parish just on the fringes of South Belfast, called Seymour Hill, a large – in Northern Ireland terms – Protestant, Loyalist, working-class parish, with all the problems that you would get in any large housing estate, and on top of that, the usual paramilitary activity that there was at that time. So it was a tough assignment. But I look back and I see that I learned so much from being there and I can see the hand of God in all of these things because each experience is also a preparation for the next one. I see that my nearly fourteen years in that parish was really quite a preparation for the work that I do now. I was ordained in 1976 and I went there in late 1977 and was there until 1991.

But during that time we were able to do many things, including a lot of cross-community and cross-border activity that people wouldn't have believed looking at us from outside because the particular area received a very bad, negative Loyalist press. We didn't publicise it but many relationships were formed which have been very important for both communities.

Tim Kearney: Looking at the whole question of the ordination of women, what are the particular gifts that you feel women can bring to ordained ministry?

Ruth Patterson: I'm always a little bit hesitant about answering that because I believe that some men can have these gifts as well and I believe a ministry composed entirely of women would be lopsided just as a ministry composed entirely of men is. But having said that, I do feel that women are, at times, more intuitive and therefore can pick up the whole pastoral scene if there is a problem. They are also maybe able to express more readily a sense of compassion and of empathy. Maybe because, in general, they find it a little bit easier to be open, and people find it easier to be more open with them in the whole pastoral scene. In terms of all the other things that you do, I remember at the beginning people saying, 'Do you do funerals?', and I'd say 'Of course I do funerals', and then they'd say 'Well, do you not cry at funerals?' And there is an assumption that a woman will cry and a man won't. I think more men should cry. I would say, 'Well, no, I don't cry because I'm there as a channel of compassion and understanding for people in a bereaved situation and I'm not there to sit down and just dissolve into tears'.

Tim Kearney: Do you welcome the development of women being called to ordained ministry within some other Christian traditions?

Ruth Patterson: Oh yes, I do. I think it's very important. I don't think that women will ever flood the Church out because, actually, it's still made very difficult for them. Certainly within our tradition, it's still difficult. Not so much from the people who teach and train but from younger male colleagues, and I think that is partially a reflection of what's been happening in Ireland over the last years. People who were a little bit tight theologically and so on, when the Troubles started, became more so, and not only hardened politically but also theologically and psychologically, in terms of relationship. So it's a tough road to travel and the ministry of priesthood anyway is a tough road if you're seeking to live it fully. One of the traps is to fall into the 'people pleasing' syndrome, which is fatal, because you can't and, in the end, you have to learn, usually the hard way, that you're not called to please men and women, you are called to please God. That's a continual lesson to learn. And a demanding one.

Tim Kearney: Would you welcome the development of ordained ministry for women within the Roman Catholic tradition?

Ruth Patterson: Yes, I would love to see that day and I think that there are so many, many good women within the Catholic Church who could fulfil that function very well. I don't think that it will come very soon but I would like to think that it would.

I think that married clergy will come first within the Catholic Church and then perhaps women priests. I wouldn't like to see this happen just because there are falling numbers in the priesthood and rather than not have any, let's have some women. I would like it that women would be welcomed for their own sake.

Having said that, I'm uneasy with any extreme feminist movement. I can see why it has developed out of an insecurity, maybe because of a hard struggle, but I think that is just as off-putting and I would go so far as to say, as wrong, as an extreme male chauvinism. I think it does more damage to the whole Good News than helps in any way.

Tim Kearney: What, in your opinion, is the core value of Christian spirituality?

Ruth Patterson: When I think of the core of Christianity, the verse that comes to mind is 'Look onto Jesus, on whom our faith depends from beginning to end'. So, I think it is probably faithfulness to him, to the person of Jesus. And out of that faithfulness, there then springs, hopefully, a joyful obedience and a love.

Tim Kearney: How is that faithfulness to Jesus lived out?

Ruth Patterson: First and foremost, in relationship with him, in spending time with him, quality time if you like, at which we all can be very bad. Just that special time for friendship to grow and out of that then all our other work springs. I know that Jean Vanier talks a lot about resting in Jesus and letting Jesus rest in you and I think that this is so important because it is a friendship beyond words. It's a time that is special and I feel that it is this sort of relationship that will then produce the prophetic stance and the prophetic voice that Ireland and the world needs more than anything else.

We've had everything else and this, in a sense, is part of God's upside-down Kingdom, that out of the little ones who listen and are willing to allow that friendship to grow, in hiddenness, and in the darkness very often comes strength, and out of that comes the power that is so different from the world's power.

Tim Kearney: What, in your view, is the key to living an
                 authentic spirituality in our modern world
                 today?

Ruth Patterson: I think that there are so many voices and so
                 many things seeking to pull us this way and the
                 other way, and so many solutions that are
                 offered, and so many different attractions that it's
                 so important to be focused, and to be focused to
                 hear, not all sorts of different words, but to hear
                 the word of Jesus, to listen to him, to be present
                 with him and to have him be present in us. That
                 for me is the core. I have, in a sense, nothing to
                 give without that. But with him, I have
                 everything to offer, and also from him everything
                 to receive in that sense.

                 And, the more I travel, and I know I'm a
                 pretty poor pilgrim in all of this, the more I go
                 along, I realise that I really can't take another step
                 or take another breath unless he gives me power
                 and that anything that I have to offer in my
                 ministry comes from this, the life of being
                 present with him. I find that increasingly
                 important because over the last years, especially
                 being so involved in Northern Ireland and in the
                 parish ministry and then reconciliation work,
                 I've become so aware of the very active presence
                 of evil and I often think it very strange that the
                 Church has such difficulty in even recognising
                 this when Jesus had no difficulty at all in
                 recognising and naming Satan for who he was
                 and what he was about.

                 It's become very obvious to me and I think
                 to many others that, for example, what's been
                 happening to us in Northern Ireland in the last
                 years has not been just a battle between people,

but that we've been wrestling with principalities and powers.

Sometimes I used to think that there was so much effort poured into all sorts of peace movements and so much heroic self-sacrifice and relatively little came out the other end. I think one of the reasons was that we hadn't named the real enemy. Whenever you name something, it loses some of its power over you. Not recognising and not naming him, we hadn't looked at the right weapons for fighting him, which we find in the New Testament in terms of the spiritual armour and praying at all times.

Then we wonder why the Church is ineffective and I think one of the reasons is that we haven't recognised this particular force which, as I say, Jesus had no difficulty recognising. And so we're trapped. A friend of mine once said, the way the devil works best is to innoculate people with a small dose of Christianity to prevent them catching the real thing.

I think that, perhaps, partially the problem with the Churches is that we've got a small dose and we've been innoculated from the real thing, so we're not living the Good News the way it should be, and Satan is very subtle. If he wasn't we'd have no difficulty recognising him and we'd reject him, but he knows our Achilles' Heel – both our individual and our communal ones – and he knows exactly where to get us, in very subtle and attractive ways. So we need to know, firstly, how to recognise and then, not only to stand against, but sometimes to go out on the offensive against those forces that are seeking to trap and imprison us and imprison the Church of Jesus Christ.

Tim Kearney: How would you see that happening, going on
                    the offensive? In practical ways or practical
                    terms, how would you envisage that?

Ruth Patterson: Well, again I think the basic ways are an effective
                    prayer life, so that our wisdom and our
                    discernment and everything else will increase and
                    sharpen, and then our action is prayer-
                    motivated. Obviously that will take each person
                    in a different direction, into areas of justice and
                    all these other areas, different paths. But also
                    being courageous enough to be able to recognise
                    and name where evil exists directly, as well as evil
                    in structures, and everything else.

Tim Kearney: Just to finish up, it would be good if you might
                    share a few words about your current ministry,
                    which is in Restoration Ministries. What is the
                    core of this ministry?

Ruth Patterson: Restoration Ministries was formed in Belfast
                    about ten years ago but it's really only in the last
                    few years that we seem to have taken off. You
                    know, it always takes a little while.
                        We take our name from the twenty-third
                    Psalm, 'He restores my soul'. The Ministry has
                    two main thrusts, healing and reconciliation,
                    although I've come to see in recent years that
                    reconciliation is, in itself, a form of healing.
                        Our calling is to be present with people who
                    have in any way been victimised or trapped by
                    either their personal or communal problems, both
                    in the Irish context and beyond. So that work
                    takes several forms. The private unpublicised
                    confidential work where people come to see us, to
                    tell their story, to be heard and to be prayed with.
                    We like to think we provide a safe place for people

to do that. That is very important. There are so many people needing to give voice to some of the things that have happened to them in their lives, especially through the last thirty years. It's like a silent scream arising from the heart of Ireland that needs to be given voice. A lot of our problems won't be laid to rest until those voices are heard and then people can lay something down and move on.

It's also important that it's safe. In Ireland there are so many face-to-face relationships and so little confidentiality, sadly often within the Church. So we don't keep records on who comes here and we always say to people 'if anybody finds out that you've come it's because you've chosen to tell them'. And very often they do, because they have found encouragement or help. So there is real confidentiality and a safe place created here and that's so important. Central to our life and work here is prayer and every day we stop at twelve noon and we pray for peace in Ireland and peace in the world and for everybody who has asked us to pray for them.

A more public side of the work is that we run a lot of seminars and courses on a short and sharp basis rather than people enrolling for a winter or whatever. We run courses like Restoring Wholeness, highlighting for people how they can be trapped by their individual or national past and how they can be freed up and how God can set them along the road towards greater freedom and wholeness. We look at all sorts of things, like stuff we've inherited, like unforgiveness and what that does to us, our reaction and attitudes and so on. We do another course on looking at the Beatitudes as principles of Kingdom-living. This last year we developed one on Restoring Hospitality, not only God's welcome of us but also how we welcome back the unacknowledged parts within ourselves. Also welcoming the stranger, and the journey to, and the final welcome of, death.

We also run a monthly meeting. We don't run a weekly one as we don't want to be drawing people away from their own communities and Churches. We take a theme for the year and this year it's 'A Shared Journey'. In all humility, we are about restoring the Church rather than creating yet another one. In that sense we exist almost to give ourselves away. We also seek in every way we can to provide opportunities for people to build bridges between each other and establish relationships, so we throw a lot of open houses. We often have a lot of guests staying here and when they are here we would throw an open house for people to come in. That has two purposes, one so that our visitors may meet local people but also that local people may meet each other in a safe place.

We then have a lot of people who would contact us because they either want to know what's going on here in Northern Ireland, in general, or in terms of reconciliation and healing. I travel the country a lot speaking about the importance of peace and reconciliation and healing. We work with volunteers largely. I'm the only full-time person. We don't have the resources to do anything else but we've got a good team of thirty to forty volunteers, a part-time secretary, and now a list of friends of the Ministry, who number about six hundred and who are all over the world.

*A native of Cork, **Danny Canty** has been a member of the L'Arche community in Cork since 1986. He works in the L'Arche workshop and his work activities include woodwork, gardening and lifeskills. He loves working with his hands and he has a great interest in history. He is a passionate collector of flags. He currently lives in a house in the L'Arche community.*

On the Internet with Flags

An Interview with Danny Canty, 1999

Tim Kearney: Danny, tell me about your story before you came to L'Arche.

Danny Canty: I originally come from Cork. I was born in St Finbarr's Hospital and my full name is Daniel John Canty. I was born in 1963. I used to go to school in St Vincent's and the teachers said that I wasn't fit for the school because I had a learning disability. They didn't want me there. So I went down to Cope Foundation on the Mardyke – that was a special school. I was only seven years of age and that was 1969. That was thirty years ago when I went to that school. I liked it.

       Then I went to Montenotte to Scoil Bernadette. I left there when I was sixteen years old and went to the VTC – the Vocational Training Centre – and I loved it. I met loads of people there. I was doing woodwork and metalwork and other things. After that I went working in a hotel, Arbutus Lodge Hotel. Afterwards then I left that too. It wasn't a fit job for me. Then I went to Cope in Hollyhill. I didn't get on with one of the people there, one of the supervisors, he was kinda a bit bossy. Afterwards then I went to Our Lady's Psychiatric Hospital.

Tim Kearney: Why did you have to go there?

Danny Canty: Because I had no friends and I was very lonely at home and my parents found me very hard to manage. Because I was getting a lot of breakdowns and I was getting into a lot of tantrums, temper tantrums. I got angry, my life was in a mess really.

Tim Kearney: How did you get on in Our Lady's?

Danny Canty: I got on OK but I found it very hard. Because the place was not clean. It was very dirty. There were flies everywhere and mice and the whole place was just like prison. A prison like in the Middle Ages.

Tim Kearney: Were the staff good to you?

Danny Canty: Some of them were and some of them weren't. After Our Lady's then I went to St Anne's, another hospital. Because I was working in the Rehab on the Douglas Road. I got myself into trouble there, in the Rehab, and got sent to St Anne's.
                  Then I got a turn, a fit – because I was on heavy medication. My Dad was very worried about me, because I was falling down on the floor and I had a reaction from the medication. I was getting turns. So then I went down to a different hospital, Sarsfield's Court.

Tim Kearney: How did you get on there?

Danny Canty: I was on Block 4 and that was a very good place because I got on great with some of the patients.

They were very good to me, they used to give me ice-cream. I was nearly spoilt down there. The nurses weren't all that good.

Tim Kearney: Did you get out of there after a while?

Danny Canty: I did. And that was the end of hospital for the time being. But what happened then, I got a bit sick again and my parents brought me to Our Lady's again and St Anne's and I got a turn up in St Anne's and they had to bring me into the Sick Ward for an injection. After that I went back up to Our Lady's. I missed my parents. My mother came every night to visit me. I was in my pyjamas, the nurse opened the door with the key and it freaked me out because the doors were locked and you couldn't go out for a walk or anything. It was terrible. It was really an institution, and I found it very hard. I was isolated. It was like a prison. It was like being in the Maze in Belfast or Mountjoy in Dublin. Because you can't come out, without keys. I was being abused really. It was not my parents' fault because they thought they were doing right, but they didn't know it was like hell.

Tim Kearney: How did you find out about L'Arche?

Danny Canty: My Mother and Father had gone out one morning and they heard the radio and yourself and Donie were on the radio. Donie was talking about L'Arche and how people like each other and how it was a place to live. And it was very hard for me to get a place where people cared about me. I tried everywhere. But then my Mother heard Donie and she said 'that could be a good place for Danny'. And after that, myself and my Dad went over to see it. We rang at the bell and you came out and you gave me a good handshake. I was only twenty-three years of age. Then I met Eugene, Kate and Mary Mac. I was very welcomed. Then both my mother and Dad said 'that could be a good place for Danny'.

Tim Kearney: How did you feel about that?

Danny Canty: All right. I wasn't sure how I felt. Would I trust the place? But my trust was building up. At the start I used to work in the community one day a week. I used to get the bus out every week. And then, after a while, I'd come to the community every weekend and stay. I got to like it. Thirteen years I'm living there now.

Tim Kearney: Was it 1986 when you first came to live in the community?

Danny Canty: Yes, I moved in on the 6th of January, 1986, the Feast of the Epiphany, Little Christmas. I really like that time of the year. My Mum and Dad came out with me. We had a little celebration and I got a present. I was really happy.

Tim Kearney: Did you find it hard to adapt to community life?

Danny Canty: In the start I found it very hard, very strange. I missed my Mum and Dad and I missed things. I used to get a lot of tantrums too in the beginning. I broke a window in An Croí, the house I was living in.

Tim Kearney: How long did it take you to settle down properly?

Danny Canty: Nearly two years, a long time. I was very isolated on account of what happened to me in the past.

Tim Kearney: What for you are the hard things about living in community?

Danny Canty: Sometimes I don't like fighting. Sometimes I have disagreements over something. That's hard.

Tim Kearney: Is there anything else that is hard about living in community for you?

Danny Canty: Sometimes it's hard for me when I make people disappointed. Sometimes when I hurt people. That's hard for me because I know I've done wrong. I find it very sad when people leave. I find it very hard to say goodbye to people that we are close to. It makes me sad.

Tim Kearney: When assistants come and stay a year and then leave, that makes you sad?

Danny Canty: It makes me very sad because I get close to them.

Tim Kearney: What for you are the good things about living in community?

Danny Canty: Different things, like yourself now, welcoming me into your home with your children. Because I like children so much, they make me happy, and you to welcome me here to your home, and your wife. I enjoy that. I enjoy coming down to the country, I like the country. I enjoy the quietness. In the city there is noise. I like visiting people. I like going out with the assistants, like Hannah. She takes me out for a cup of coffee.

Tim Kearney: Do you like welcoming people to the community?

Danny Canty: I do, I like welcoming people. Especially people from Eastern Europe. People from Poland and Hungary, people from Croatia and former Yugoslavia. At the moment we have no person from the ex-Soviet Union.

Tim Kearney: What are the other things you like about living in community?

Danny Canty: I like prayer. I like to say prayers. I don't like seeing people suffer. There was a death in the community recently, one of the core members lost their mother. She was a good friend of mine. Hannah Burchill was her name.

Tim Kearney: What work do you do in L'Arche?

Danny Canty: I work in the garden. I used to do it on Thursdays but it's changed. I'm now doing the computer in Lifeskills as well. I really really love the computer and I do a lot on the Internet with flags of different countries.
                  I do my life story on the computer, about my personal life, about my ex-girlfriends, and about the people who were in my life, in Cope and in school.

Tim Kearney: What for you is the secret of being happy and contented as a person?

Danny Canty: What makes me happy is seeing my friends. My friends in the community make me happy. I like animals.

Tim Kearney: You mentioned earlier that prayer is important
                  for you. Why?

Danny Canty: Sometimes it's good to pray to God because God
                  helps you and your Guardian Angel will protect
                  you because sometimes the evil one upsets you.
                  Some people think it's rubbish, when you talk
                  about the devil. The devil puts things in our
                  heads and sometimes he wants us unhappy. But
                  God is there and God is strong. God is stronger
                  than the devil. Sometimes when we are unhappy
                  in our lives and we think things are bad, that can
                  be the devil putting things in our heads.

Tim Kearney: You pray very often for peace in the world,
                  especially for people who are suffering in such
                  places as Kosovo, Yugoslavia and Northern
                  Ireland. Would you like to see peace in the
                  North?

Danny Canty: I would, because up in Northern Ireland they are
                  suffering so much at the moment because of
                  their different nationalities. Like the Catholics
                  and the Protestants. Some day I'd like to see
                  them getting on, shaking hands and saying
                  'Look, you can have the ground'. The Catholics
                  should say to the Orange People, 'You can march
                  there if you want to'. Not to be fighting over a
                  piece of ground. That's not nice at all, fighting
                  over a piece of ground. Life is so precious. I want
                  to see peace up there. I don't want to see
                  violence.

Tim Kearney: Do you think peace will come to the North?

Danny Canty: At the moment I'm doubting it because of the talks, you know. But it might come eventually.

Tim Kearney: You were up in Belfast recently giving a talk about the plans for a L'Arche community starting there. Are you happy that L'Arche is coming to Northern Ireland now?

Danny Canty: I am. I am very happy that L'Arche is coming there. It's good to have it coming there.

Tim Kearney: What is your hope for humanity in the new millennium?

Danny Canty: That there be peace between different countries and I hope in the new millennium that Eastern Europe will go into the EEC, be a part of the EU because they need it, you know. Because when communism collapsed they lost everything. They lost money and everything.

Therese Vanier, a Canadian, was born in England in 1923. She was educated in England, where she went on to study and practise medicine. In 1972 she left a conventional medical career to work in palliative medicine (St Christopher's Hospice) as well as establish L'Arche communities in the UK. She has contributed to the development of palliative care in France, Belgium and Switzerland through frequent visits and lectures. She retired from medical practice in 1988 and remains a member of L'Arche Lambeth in London. She continues to have a particular concern for the ecumenical aspects of L'Arche and for the needs of long-term assistants.

UNLIKELY GIVERS?

An Interview with Therese Vanier, 1999

Tim Kearney: When your brother Jean first announced to the family that he was starting L'Arche and had decided to live with two men with a learning disability in a small village in Northern France, what was your own personal reaction?

Therese Vanier: I think my predominant reaction was one of great interest. Jean had changed his vocation or his career quite a number of times and he didn't do these things, on the whole, without quite a lot of reflection. I found it very interesting and I think looking back on it, why I found it interesting was that I was searching for something more comprehensive in my care of patients at the time myself.

Tim Kearney: Where were you working at that time?

Therese Vanier: In 1964 I was a clinical haematologist at St Thomas's Hospital in London. I had recently spent two years in Boston training as a paediatric haematologist.

Tim Kearney: So what Jean was doing in some way connected
                  with your own search for a more comprehensive
                  approach?

Therese Vanier: I've come to the conclusion that it probably was
                  that. I went over and spent the first Christmas
                  with him and his people. I was very touched.
                  Jean met me at the train station and on the way
                  back – it had been snowing – we passed a man
                  sitting on the roadside and Jean said, 'You know
                  that chap was there when I went to collect you. I
                  think I'm going to stop and ask him if he wants
                  to come and have dinner.' So we did and he
                  accepted and his name was Gabriel. He had
                  lunch and met the other two 'archangels', Michel
                  and Raphael. Philippe was also there at the time,
                  and Michel was another resident Jean welcomed
                  at the very beginning, with whom things didn't
                  work out. Anyway, Gabriel stayed on and spent
                  the night and relationships survived, more or less,
                  until the next day when he smashed a plate on
                  Raphael's head and left. That was the beginning
                  of learning that you cannot be too inclusive, that
                  you have to have boundaries somewhere.

Tim Kearney: You were one of the founding figures of L'Arche
                  in the UK, being the Founding Director of
                  L'Arche Kent in 1974 and the Founding Director
                  of L'Arche Lambeth in London in 1977. How
                  did you get involved in L'Arche yourself in the
                  first place?

Therese Vanier: My interest in what Jean was doing continued. I
                  was very busy working, so I didn't spend much
                  time in Trosly. The Faith and Light pilgrimage to
                  Lourdes in 1971 was what actually got me

involved because I went, rather reluctantly let it be said, as the doctor with one of the groups from the London area, which incorporated people from Wales as well. I found myself spending a lot of time with two people, Billy Saunders and his elderly mother. Billy was in his early fifties and his mother was in her eighties. He was mentally handicapped and living in a hospital in South Wales. Both he and his mother were sick people. He had bad attacks of asthma and his mother had heart disease. Both of them were very overweight so most of the time they were in wheelchairs.

I was caring for them medically, which was the job I had undertaken for the group, but listening to them I realised that I could in no way meet their much deeper needs because Billy's prayer, always out loud, was, 'I don't want to go back to hospital', and his mother's prayer was, 'I don't want to die before Billy dies because if I die nobody will visit him', sometimes out loud, and also she talked to me quite a bit. What could I do? To cut a long story short, we came back and I saw Billy and his mother off to Wales. I can't say that I forgot about them but I was very busy doing other things and several weeks later I met a priest who had been in the same group, and he said, 'Have you heard about Billy?' I said 'No, what's happened to Billy?' He said, 'Well, they got back to his mother's house and it was too late to take him back to the hospital, he had an attack of asthma and before anyone could get to him he died.' So in a mysterious way, both their prayers had been answered. I'm quite sure that was what made me really reconsider what I was doing with my life. It also coincided, and I think this was quite important for me, with a deep sense that I wasn't caring properly for patients who were dying … within a big general hospital. So I started going to St Christopher's Hospice which had opened in 1968, going there at odd times to try to learn a bit more.

By that time I was seriously considering moving away from a conventional medical career. This was around 1971. I went to see an old priest in Liverpool called Fr Pownall who was a great character and also a saintly man, and I said, 'Look, I'm pretty sure this is what I ought to be doing but you know, one of these options of taking up palliative care is much more attractive to me than the L'Arche option – I know I have to be involved in one or the other and I wonder if you could help me to see which it might be.' He listened to my babbling and then said, 'You know Therese, I can't tell which it's going to be or should be, all I can say to you is whatever you decide, let it be a place where you use poor means.'

So I went back to London and the train kept saying 'use poor means, use poor means', so I was then pretty convinced that it needed to be L'Arche. I had absolutely nothing to bring to L'Arche in terms of medical care; the only mentally handicapped person I had met was Billy and he was dead. So that was the place in which I was going to use 'poor means', much more than if I was going to work in the Hospice context. The strange thing was, I handed in my notice to St Thomas's where I was working – it had to be a year's notice – and continued to go to St Christopher's. At the same time, I started setting up L'Arche in the UK. Halfway through the following year, St Christopher's said, 'Is there any way that you could do a part-time job here because we really need another doctor?' So I started working there two days a week, which actually enabled me to go on living, because I needed to find a salary.

Tim Kearney: This was before you founded L'Arche in Kent? Were you able to continue your part-time work in St Christopher's after you founded the house, Little Ewell, in 1973?

Therese Vanier: Yes, I worked for seventeen years at St Christopher's while I was in L'Arche. It kept me sane frankly, because at least I knew what I was doing there!

Tim Kearney: Both L'Arche and Hospice have been an important part of your journey. Do you see any parallels between the vision of L'Arche and the vision of the Hospice Movement?

Therese Vanier: I see a lot of parallels actually. I think there are a lot of parallels in the way they began and the way they spread to different countries. They began in the same way, I think, which was through somebody listening very carefully to some very fragile and vulnerable people. Jean started listening to mentally handicapped men and Cecily Saunders started listening to dying people when she was a social worker and a nurse and then when she was a doctor. I think that is absolutely crucial because although Christianity is dotted with people who have done things for the poor, I'm pretty convinced that the way of listening to people's needs was rather different in these cases and in many others, for I think this is part of a much wider movement.

Tim Kearney: A listening that was different in what way?

Therese Vanier: Beginning to value the person as a person rather
                    than a 'poor person' for whom I should be doing
                    something. I know that's fairly standard jargon
                    but that's really what I mean, a very careful
                    listening and a listening to things that are not
                    being said and so on. That was one common
                    characteristic.

                    The second obvious one is a very strong
                    Christian ethos carrying the vision of what
                    needed to be done. Then the third one would be
                    the completely central position of the people that
                    you're caring for within your community. The
                    dying patient and their family are central to the
                    community of St Christopher's and the
                    handicapped people are central to the
                    community of L'Arche, and very consciously so.
                    But I think more than that, a recognition very
                    early on of their giftedness, or an expression that
                    I like to use, which is 'unlikely givers'. These are
                    not people who are constantly on the receiving
                    end. They have something very important to give
                    and that something is directly linked to their
                    dependence and vulnerability.

                    So, I would suggest those four things are very
                    similar, and then the other thing of course is
                    partly the effect of globalisation. Rapid
                    communication meant that they both spread all
                    over the world in a way that wouldn't have been
                    possible fifty years ago but was possible thirty
                    years ago.

Tim Kearney: Which would explain why the vision of L'Arche
                    and the Hospice Movement has become
                    internationalised in many ways. 'Unlikely

givers'… in the context of L'Arche, what would you see as being some of the things that people with learning disabilities have given or can give, in your own experience of working with them?

Therese Vanier: For example: Gilles le Cardinal of the L'Arche community in Compiègne, France, tells the story of a man with a learning disability in the community. He was being considered for independent living but Gilles was having difficulty understanding why this man was so anxious since he was pretty competent. But the whole question of living on his own was making him more and more worried. Eventually, it came out that he really didn't think that he could do anything on his own, so Gilles asked him, 'Well what are the things you think you won't be able to do?', and he listed them. Now Gilles said, 'So if you find you can't do those things when you're living on your own, what are you going to do?'

And this chap thought for a time and then he said, 'Well, I'll ask Odile and if she's not around I'll ask Jacqueline and then there is always Mr Dubois.' So negotiations continued with him on that basis. This changed the criteria needed before someone was considered for a more independent living situation, with the addition of 'not only willing, but able to ask for help'.

Another example: years ago when I was Regional Co-ordinator and visiting the community in Kent, I sat down with Jane, who has Down's Syndrome, and said, 'Jane, what do you find good and what do you find really hard living in this community and this house?' And Jane thought for a time and she said, in her deep voice, 'I find it very difficult to love everybody.' I said, 'Well Jane, that is exactly the same problem that I have, so what do you think we can do about it', and she said, 'We just go on trying!'

Tim Kearney: The L'Arche vocation and your Hospice vocation have gone hand in hand, by and large. Would you say that you were able to live both those commitments harmoniously during those years?

Therese Vanier: Yes, it was hard work, but in the Hospice I had the privilege of just working as a doctor. I didn't have to worry whether X was speaking to Y or whether Y was on bad terms with Z, which I had to bother with in L'Arche, so it was a splendid existence to come in and see patients and then walk out again. It had its stresses but by that time the Hospice world had understood the importance of multi-disciplinary teamwork and what working as a team actually meant and so one constantly felt supported by a team that was not necessarily finding it easy to work together but had determined the absolute need to do so.

Tim Kearney: It's interesting that the same notion of multi-disciplinary teamwork also became very current in L'Arche. To move on a little bit, one of the things this book is exploring is the way in which people with learning disabilities can be prophetic. Would you agree with this and, if so, in what ways would you see them as being prophetic?

Therese Vanier: I have difficulty with that word, it's a little bit like the word 'the poor', it's OK in French but in English it's difficult to translate. I don't like the word prophetic in this context because I don't

really know what it means but for me the value of
people with mental handicaps in our society and
in our Churches, is that they are people who
operate at the level of the heart. Whereas the rest
of humanity tends, on the whole, to be not too
sure what its heart is doing but listens to the head
and operates at the level of the head. The life of
the heart is very marked in people with mental
handicaps, because of their extraordinary
dependence on others. They can help society to
achieve some sort of balance, if they are allowed
to do so. Of course, the same can be said of dying
people and the same can be said of small
children, and of many others whose vulnerability
is manifest.

Tim Kearney: A balance on what level?

Therese Vanier: Between the heart and the head. Re-establishing
some sort of balance because it seems to me that
Western civilisation anyway – I don't know about
the rest of the world – is moving more and more
into the head, into a technological empire of
rapid communication and rapid everything, but
where any sense of what it means to be human is
being lost.

Tim Kearney: Do you feel that people with learning disabilities
have something to teach us or say to us in that
regard?

Therese Vanier: They surely have and you make that point very
strongly and Jean makes it very strongly: the
whole question of these people helping us to see
what it means to be human. Of course, it's not
always very pleasant being human, it can be a

very painful experience, and so being alongside people who are constantly blurting out to you what it means to be human is a very uncomfortable experience. It's the same uncomfortable experience if you are a doctor and you can't save the life of a patient. We defend ourselves when we are confronted with what resonates with our own pain, we defend ourselves in all sorts of different ways and one of the ways is simply to close off the relationship and by-pass it – hence the 'uncaring doctor', who can't talk to patients when they are seriously ill and may walk past the end of the bed, and so on.

Tim Kearney: Whereas the call is to be present to people in their pain and in their humanity?

Therese Vanier: Not only that but to understand what is going on in this relationship. This is something that I feel very, very strongly about. I don't think that we articulate it or understand why it is that for years and years people with mental handicaps were shut away and that dying people were shut away.

Tim Kearney: So it's something to do with the expression of their humanity resonating with our own humanity in ways that aren't comfortable?

Therese Vanier: That are very uncomfortable. Of course the other side of that is the enormous comfort one can get if one is willing to enter into such a relationship.

Tim Kearney: Moving on now to the question of L'Arche and its dual identity as a professional service provider and a faith community. What is the most important challenge facing L'Arche today in that regard?

Therese Vanier: I think it's a question of how we move from the
                    heroic to the humdrum and that we stop
                    operating at the 'adrenaline fix' level all the time.
                    I know there are a whole lot of implications in
                    that sort of vague statement.

                    It's about slowing down, it's about a much
                    greater understanding of what is going on. It's a
                    greater understanding of what it means to be a
                    house-leader for example and how we can ask the
                    impossible of house-assistants living in big houses
                    with very dependent people.

                    I must say I get pretty exasperated because of
                    the number of times that the needs of house-
                    assistants have been analysed. Why is it we seem
                    quite incapable of doing something about it?
                    One example, which I think is quite telling,
                    relates to somebody who was the Houses Co-
                    ordinator in a community. She had never actually
                    been in charge of a house herself before becoming
                    Houses Co-ordinator. At one time she had been
                    a nurse, was in her thirties, a mature person. She
                    said she couldn't go on being Houses Co-
                    ordinator with house-leaders changing every year,
                    and she has taken charge of one of the big houses
                    herself. Her comment after six months of being
                    house-leader was something to the effect that 'I
                    had no idea how much people have to do'. At
                    least here is a beginning, thirty years on: a greater
                    awareness!

Tim Kearney: Do you feel the two aspects of faith community
                    and service provider are compatible?

Therese Vanier: I think they have got to be. I mean, either that or
                    we close down. So we've got to learn.

Obviously one of the reasons there is so much work for a house-leader in a L'Arche household is that very issue – we are constantly having to, in this country anyway, relate to local social services, and inspections and paperwork, registration, etc. As well as trying to have creative times of prayer, celebration and all the rest of it. It is actually almost an impossibility, unless you are extremely organised and you have people who are coming in and out and on whom you can rely to carry out specific tasks. There are ways of organising something in a way that makes it much more possible. But at the same time, I think it is actually part of our mission to be in a good relationship with the statutory authorities, because they are intrigued by us, and sometimes perhaps exasperated by us, but intrigued, nonetheless. I think that when requirements appear on the scene, we may contest them, as we have done recently in this country, about the minimum wage, and we won that particular contest. That is important, it made it possible for us to continue. My goodness, if we hadn't won that battle, I don't know what we would have done. We would have either become illegal or we would have had to lose half our assistants.

Nonetheless, the fact that we won that battle means that it forces us to say that we are an intentional community. In other words, if we stop being an intentional community, we are not going to be exempt any longer.

Some rules and regulations can be contested and we will find a way around some of the other difficulties. Yet some rules and regulations, like the ones connected with sexual abuse, are useful in that they force us to look at an issue when in our naivety we might think, 'Oh well, the way we operate, it wouldn't happen.' Of course it happens, and it has happened.

Tim Kearney: So we need to have a positive interaction with statutory authority.

Therese Vanier: We have to, and we have to find ways in which to do it. All this requires reflection, and I liked the article you wrote in the *Letters of L'Arche:* you were talking about the need for reflection, whereas in too many communities everybody is 'running around'. We have to begin to understand why this happens and do something about it, so that there is time to think.

Tim Kearney: Particularly as we live the double challenge of aspiring to be a competent service provider, engaging in a positive way with statutory authorities, and at the same time a vibrant faith community. That's a great challenge. What else do you see as being significant developments in L'Arche today?

Therese Vanier: The other thing that is important for L'Arche – and I think it is beginning, but it has taken a long time to get there – is creating something that is really coherent in terms of integrating the psychological and the spiritual. There is a reluctance to do that and more reluctance in some countries than in others, which is perfectly understandable. We really need to get to grips with the kind of dynamics that go on when you've got fragile assistants coming into community to meet their own needs. They don't know they are doing this, but they are. How many fragile people can we carry? When we are also asking them to care for people who are fragile, in similar or different ways. We need to develop an understanding of the dynamics that go on, because they are the dynamics that go on in any caring situation and we have really got to start articulating them.

Tim Kearney: What in your view is the most significant feature of the spirituality of L'Arche?

Therese Vanier: That is something that is quite difficult to be precise about. I suppose it is the opportunity of practical application of paradox. Christianity is full of paradox and rightly so because it's the human condition, where weakness and strength, the wise and foolish, go hand in hand. You can pick out any number of examples. I think that's probably one important thing in L'Arche. The other important thing is the possibility of very practically demonstrating the phenomenon of slow healing of wounded hearts and minds through faithful covenant relationships.

Tim Kearney: What do you mean by covenant relationships?

Therese Vanier: I mean faithful relationships between assistants and handicapped people. As an example, the other day at a community evening I was sitting next to a great big man, originally from the Caribbean, Mark, who's been in the community for about five years now. He is a very, very traumatised man with a learning disability. The last thing that he wants is to participate in anything to do with prayer, or anything that is quiet and peaceful. The only way to keep him quiet during prayers used to be to allow him to read his *Daily Mirror*.

So, at the community evening, I was sitting next to Mark, and the assistant who was close to him was on the other side. When it came to the prayer time Mark folded up his paper and slipped it behind his back and then opened up his hands offering them to his neighbours – we all hold hands to say the 'Our Father' – and he started the 'Our Father'. I could hardly believe it!

When I think of the number of assistants who have struggled with Mark, sometimes literally, sometimes just trying to understand what it's all about.... Yet there had been an opening up and a slow healing.

Tim Kearney: In terms of the practical application of paradox, weakness and strength, the foolish and the wise, have you any stories that embody that – in your own experience?

Therese Vanier: There's a man called Pat, who is one of the most anguished people I have ever met. He is mentally handicapped, and he has been in the community since the very beginning. About fifteen years ago, I went down with Pat and other people to the confirmation of another mentally handicapped man. Pat is terrified of certain things, stairs being one of them, and coming out of the cathedral there are very shallow stairs. Pat was about to embark on a panic attack, and I firmly took his hand and distracted him as best I could. Then, a man on the other side of him nearly knocked him over. Pat righted himself and realised that the man was going to fall. So he took the man's hand. At that point I realised that Pat was completely distracted from the stairs, so I let go of his hand. He then helped this man, who was drunk, to come down the steps. Then the man sat down on one of the steps, so Pat sat next to him and just looked at him and said, 'My name is Pat, what's your name?' The man didn't answer, he was past it.

So Pat went on chatting to him. I didn't think this could go on indefinitely so I said, 'Pat, we're going to miss our bus, I think we'd better be off. You know you have helped this man down and he's OK now on the steps.' And then Pat turned to the man and said (and sometimes he gets his genders mixed up), 'He's in a hurry, sorry I've got to go.'

What did I learn from that when I thought about it? I am frightened of drunken men on the streets, when I see one coming I cross over. Why am I afraid of them? Certainly one of the reasons is that I don't want to enter into any sort of relationship where I'm going to be asked something by somebody who I really can't tolerate. Pat's an example of how one can avoid being over-involved!

Tim Kearney: Looking at the Christian Churches in the world today, what do you see as their greatest challenge, in the context of our modern world?

Therese Vanier: I believe that the presence of very vulnerable people in a group can either have a very destructive effect or can have a salvific effect, depending on how they are treated.

If I really believe that, then I think I've got to say the same about the Christian Churches. So everything that I've said about what L'Arche needs to look at, the place of people with mental handicap and so on, I would apply to the Churches.

If I wanted to say something that would really make people think I was slightly mad, I'd say the Churches need to start rebuilding, to start rebuilding from where unexpected life and creativity is to be found.

Tim Kearney: Can you give any concrete examples?

Therese Vanier: Well, it's a question of the Churches being more conciliatory, reconciling rather than polarising. Cardinal Hume was a very, very good example of this. The way he was trying to keep the two poles, the left and the right of the Church, together. Cardinal Bernadin in the United States was trying to do the same thing. Can we not move towards a more human approach and try to get away from the oppressive kind of authoritarian, rigid stance? I'm very interested and very influenced by the books of Kevin Kelly, who is a moral theologian.

He and a number of other theologians are forming a group of people who are spending time listening to very vulnerable people and beginning to rethink moral theology, in what Kevin Kelly describes as 'the light of the challenge of being human'. He has been very carefully listening to people, and people with AIDS in particular.

Tim Kearney: So, Cardinal Hume then would have been one of those people who, for you, embodied that commitment and ability to reconcile?

Therese Vanier: To put the primacy on reconciliation and listening rather than on dogma and condemnation. The implications of that are simple in a sense. It's a question of helping people to be more human, and that begins in the seminary, with the whole area of training and formation and interpersonal relationships.

Tim Kearney: What would you consider the key to living an authentic spirituality in our modern world?

Therese Vanier: I think of spirituality as meaning the spirit in which I try to live ... in which people try to live. For me there are three key elements. The first is honesty and self-knowledge, which really means integrity, some integrity between what you say and what you do. And secondly, doing it together. In a world of individualism it is impossible to live any kind of integrated spirituality on one's own.

Tim Kearney: So doing it together would imply a sense of community?

Therese Vanier: Yes, a community, a network, whatever. The third element is that of companioning, or accompaniment, as we call it in L'Arche. You can't be working in a group of people, doing things together, sharing things, without a mentor who can guide and listen to individuals and help people to articulate what they experience.

Tim Kearney: What for you is the core value of Christian spirituality? Is there any one particular thread that you'd like to pull out and say, well, for me, this is it. For some people it might be hospitality, for others it might be compassion, what is it for you?

Therese Vanier: I suppose it is the whole question of the life that emerges through death, which is a paradox.

Within that, again, you've got the question of the kingdom values, the Beatitudes, the question of death, hope, resurrection, and also very strongly I find, because it is something that comes up so often in the context of L'Arche and the Hospice world, is the so-called 'meaning' of suffering. The unwisdom of anybody pontificating about the meaning of suffering is obvious, but when you can see life growing out of suffering, you don't have to pontificate. This is the kind of thing that a theologian, like Kevin Kelly, is so good at describing. A particular example was a visit he made to the Philippines and Thailand with other moral theologians, tackling questions about AIDS and witnessing the loving creativity of some suffering from the disease in caring for others.

Those theologians spent time listening to women in particular, whose personal stories are fairly familiar in that part of the world. Although they had become infected themselves and knew they would get AIDS, they created a movement that was concentrating on caring for others with the disease. Then you don't have to pontificate about the meaning of suffering, all you can say sometimes is 'Come and see'!

Tim Kearney: So you do believe that suffering does have meaning?

Therese Vanier: I'm sure suffering has meaning, the suffering of Christ undoubtedly has meaning. What one can't do is go around telling people what the meaning is. But when people discover the meaning by what they do with their own suffering, then you need to celebrate this and say 'Come and see'.

Michael Kearney qualified in medicine from University College, Cork, in 1977. He began his training in palliative medicine in St Christopher's Hospice in London in 1980. In 1982 he spent a sabbatical year in L'Arche, Trosly-Breuil, where he worked at La Chaumière with adults with profound mental handicap. In 1983 he returned to London and continued his postgraduate training in St Thomas's Hospital, where he worked as Clinical Research Fellow with the St Thomas's Hospital Palliative Care Support Team. In 1986 he was offered a consultant post in St Christopher's Hospice. Since 1989 he has been working in Dublin as Consultant in Palliative Medicine at Our Lady's Hospice, St Vincent's Hospital, and University College, Dublin. He has been involved in developing palliative care at a European and national level. He has published widely and lectured internationally on all aspects of palliative care. He is particularly interested in psychospiritual aspects of palliative care and has written a book called Mortally Wounded, *which addresses these issues for a general readership. His second book,* A Place of Healing: Working with Suffering in Living and Dying, *will be published in June 2000.*

A PLACE OF HEALING

An Interview with Michael Kearney, 1999

Tim Kearney: You spent a sabbatical year in L'Arche Trosly, the founding L'Arche community in France, in the early Eighties. Tell me a little about that.

Michael Kearney: I had by then begun my studies in St Christopher's Hospice in London in palliative medicine – but maybe I should backtrack a step really because the connections between L'Arche and palliative care and medicine for me were, in a sense, there from the very beginning.

I was in Cork University as a medical student and I was a bit ambivalent about studying medicine. I was also interested in other areas, such as the Arts and film-making, and wasn't quite sure why I was studying medicine. When I began working on the wards of the teaching hospital, I was hoping that this would confirm it for me, but on the contrary I found what I saw there quite disillusioning. What particularly disturbed me was the attitude around people who had incurable illnesses. Those patients didn't seem to be so interesting to the doctors on their rounds and there seemed to me to be something very unfair and unjust in this. I felt disillusioned, to the point where I was actually thinking medicine wasn't for me.

It was around this time that I first heard of the work of Jean Vanier. He had given a retreat in University College, Dublin, and some people I knew were going. I decided I'd go along. In the course of this I was chatting to Jean and I was telling him about what I was doing and how I was thinking of leaving my medical studies, and he said, 'Before you leave medicine, can I suggest you do one thing, that is, to visit this hospice in London, my sister works there. It's called St Christopher's Hospice.' He added, 'It's a place of healing.' I remember that phrase, it struck me. I recalled it afterwards when I actually went there. At first glance it might seem a bit incompatible, that this hospice – this specialist unit for people with advanced and terminal illness – was 'a place of healing', but in fact when I went and spent a week there, that was very much my experience. It was a place of healing in a very deep sense, in the sense of persons becoming more whole, more complete in themselves, even as they died, surrounded by tremendous care and attention from the staff, with involvement all the way through from their families. I felt, 'Yes, this is what I want to do.' I then returned to Ireland and finished my medical studies. As soon as I could – I first had to get my postgraduate qualification under my belt – I went back and worked in St Christopher's. I was there for two years and I found it a very rewarding time.

Tim Kearney: Did that confirm your intuition that this was the right road to go?

Michael Kearney: It did confirm that intuition and it also confronted me with a whole new set of questions, not least because it was very intensive work. I was in the presence of a lot of very difficult situations, very stressful situations, and a lot of suffering. I found it very challenging.

On the one hand, I found this very rewarding, deeply rewarding, work. I really loved it, and I knew that this was what I wanted to do. On the other hand, it was taking its toll on a personal level. So I decided to take some time out as I needed time to reflect on all that had been happening and to make decisions on the future direction of my work. That's how I came to decide to spend a sabbatical year in L'Arche, Trosly.

Tim Kearney: What sort of a year was it for you? Did it give you that reflective space you needed in terms of looking at the future?

Michael Kearney: It did and it was a totally different rhythm. I had a two-hour lunch break with my family as opposed to ten minutes in the cafeteria of the hospital! I also found it very challenging. I didn't speak French when I went there but it wasn't just that I had to learn a new language in an oral sense; it was like I had to learn a completely new language at another level. This had to do with a way of working and being with people.

Tim Kearney: Can you say more about this?

Michael Kearney: In everyday medical work the emphasis is on problem-solving, investigating, analysing, intervening, doing, 'making better' and, sometimes, making life and death decisions, which have immediate consequences.

By contrast, in this situation, I was getting to know and spending time with just a few people who had very serious handicaps, who weren't able to communicate verbally and who often had a lot of self-directed violence, which I found very difficult and which I wasn't sure how to handle. And there weren't any answers – there weren't problems to be solved! This was the real culture shock – it confronted me with a sense of redundancy and impotence. Not being able to speak French was really just a metaphor for my inability to be with these people.

The 'new' language was about finding a way of being with another in suffering and this brought me into my own suffering also. It was about staying in suffering together, of finding a way of being in suffering together in a way that brought some kind of healing and peace.

Tim Kearney: How did this time in Trosly impact on your spiritual journey?

Michael Kearney: In a number of ways. All in all the experience was an endorsement of the inner world and the inner life. And L'Arche taught me something important about the healing potential of being in suffering. Of being in suffering with another, of what can happen if we stay in that place together, believing that somehow, something can happen through that experience which is beyond the sum of the two persons in the relationship.

Tim Kearney: Do you think that insight in some way was important for you then in your subsequent work, when you chose, after this year in L'Arche Trosly, to return to the world of Hospice and your career as a doctor in the context of Hospice. Did that vision of healing and the potential healing of being in suffering with another carry over in some way then?

Michael Kearney: Yes. This has influenced how I've approached my work and what I see as important for me in the work I do, and more recently what I have written about and what I teach about. I came back from that year in France and I completed my training in palliative care. I had decided after that year that palliative or hospice care was what I really wanted to do. Having completed my training, I worked in St Christopher's Hospice in London as a consultant for a couple of years.

During that time, one of the areas I was particularly interested in developing was education programmes to teach healthcare professionals the importance of who they are and not just what they do; not setting up some kind of a comparison or making a value judgement between those two poles but recognising that as carers we are both. We are what we know and what we do and we are, also, who we are as persons. The fact of the matter is that, particularly in medical education and in health care in general, who we are as persons just doesn't feature in it at all. It's assumed that who we are will manifest itself at the bedside in our bedside manner. Current medical education is about teaching the facts and necessary skills. It really doesn't address the question of who the person of the carer is. With regard to this whole 'person' aspect of medicine, you won't find anybody who will say that it's not important, because everybody agrees that it is, but in terms of the current systems of medical education, it doesn't really get much space.

Tim Kearney: In your own work then, you were able to develop some training modules focusing on the importance of relationship, the importance of bringing an awareness of self to the role as well as the more obvious medical knowledge?

Michael Kearney: That's what interested me and I wanted to do it in a way that endorsed both, that says, 'Yes, it's essential that you are competent, that you are expert, that you know what to do, that you can intervene and make a difference, but it's equally important that this is in the context of the relationship, and the relationship is about who you are and who the other person is.' It's not just about setting up the relationship so that you can do your doctoring thing, or your nursing thing, or your social work thing, it's actually seeing *that the relationship itself is a place of healing.* I think this recognition is important in trying to redress the balance of medical education.

Tim Kearney: In your book, *Mortally Wounded,* you talk about
                    moving from what you call the 'traditional
                    hero/victim' model of Western medicine to the
                    notion of the doctor or carer as the 'wounded
                    healer', where both the doctor and the patient are
                    also present to each other, beyond their respective
                    roles, on a person-to-person level. This seems to
                    open the door to a different type of healing
                    process, where the emphasis is on quality of
                    relationship, vulnerability and trust. Could you
                    say more about this?

Michael Kearney: One way of looking at this is to consider the
                    related concepts of pain and suffering. Pain is
                    defined as the experience that results from
                    damage to a part. An example is someone who
                    has got cancer that has spread to the bone or the
                    liver. That person may have bone pain or liver
                    pain. The good news is that we now have
                    effective ways of treating pain and the vast
                    majority of pain can be controlled. So pain
                    necessitates an intervention from the outside to
                    make it better and relies on somebody else's
                    expertise. One could say that pain and pain
                    control is what the heroic model of Western
                    medicine is all about. It's really about problem-
                    solving, which is dependent on somebody
                    coming along with their expertise and making
                    somebody else's problems better.

                        In contrast to pain, suffering, as defined by
                    Eric Caselles, is the experience that results from
                    damage to the whole – that is, to the whole
                    person – where the intactness of the person is
                    threatened. An example of suffering is grief,
                    where one can literally feel as if one's world has
                    fallen apart and where there isn't an answer,

where there isn't an obvious fix, an obvious cure. Whereas with pain we can look for and usually find a cure, when it comes to suffering, such as grief, there is something about having to accept that there isn't an answer. Now that does not mean that one can't come through grief, but the way through grief is actually by living with one's grief until such time as one finds oneself living with it in an easier way, in a less distressed way than one did, perhaps, in the early days and weeks and months of bereavement.

At this stage one realises, 'Yes, something has changed. I can now live with my loss. I'm not saying I'm happy with it but I've found a way of living with it and in a curious way the loss has become part of who I am'. What's happening here is not that someone has come along from the outside with some expertise and made this suffering better, but that an individual has endured in their suffering until such time as a change has gradually come about within that person themselves.

So in terms of Western medicine the heroic model is very much about pain control, whereas another model is needed when it comes to being with persons in their suffering. I think calling this the 'wounded healer' model is particularly apt because being with somebody in their suffering immediately confronts one with one's own inadequacies, one's own inability to make it better, and that's a very painful place to be.

Part of what helps a person through suffering is a relationship of trust, a relationship of presence, which involves the carer staying with the person in their suffering. There is something very levelling in this experience which involves the carer realising their own suffering and being able to stay with this and, perhaps, almost in an act of faith, trusting that their being there may be of some value to the other person, even though at the time it may feel like exactly the opposite. The person in suffering may then feel that somebody is with them, that while they may still be alone in their suffering, they are no longer isolated.

This can give the person encouragement to stay with, and in, his or her experience, because the paradox seems to be that the only way through is in suffering. And so, if the person is encouraged to stay with their experience, gradually and over time, that change and that healing can come about within the individual.

Tim Kearney: So the role of relationship and of presence in that sense is significant and important?

Michael Kearney: It's crucial. In a way it creates the environment and it creates the space in which that healing can happen. Again, it's back to that word, encouragement. It literally gives the person courage to stay with their suffering and it seems to me that this is the first step towards healing. With this comes a little more openness to the experience itself. Then, within that experience, change can gradually come about.

Tim Kearney: What would you say, leading on from that, a dying person needs most from their loved ones and those around them? Obviously presence and that quality of relationship that you have evoked there in the 'wounded healer' model is something very crucial and significant?

Michael Kearney: Absolutely, and I suppose realising that again this experience doesn't always feel good. But it's very important to bear with it nonetheless, to continue to be present. To care, to give attention – that's terribly important – because I think all those things enable the person to live more fully what they are living. This is what I understand by the concept of healing, which is so different to curing. Curing is about fixing, it's about restoring the status quo. Healing is about becoming more whole, it's about integrating more fully all aspects of who we are, and in that process becoming more fully alive, becoming more human.

Tim Kearney: What in your view is the key to living an authentic spirituality in our modern world?

Michael Kearney: I think for me the first step is to recognise, as Sting puts it, that 'There's a deeper wave than this'. Recognising that what we're seeing and what we're living, while vital and important, is also the surface of a deeper reality. The recognition of that deeper reality within ourselves and within others and within the world we live in is, for me, the first step.

Flowing on from that, a recognition of the importance of committing oneself to that inner world and that inner work and recognising that for every person, the actual form and shape that it is going to take is going to be as individual and unique as they are. There can perhaps be some common patterns to things but it's also a very individual and unique process. It's an individual journey and different for each person.

The other thing that comes to mind relates to something I heard at a conference I was at recently. A Professor Costelliano, an elder in the Mohawk tribe, was talking about how, within her spiritual tradition, there is the concept of the medicine wheel, the wheel of life, and how each individual has their particular place within this.

She spoke of how we must each find what is 'our place' in the wheel of life and then commit ourselves to this. That's what we are responsible for. We're not responsible for the whole wheel but we are responsible for our own individual part of the process. So I think part of what the inner journey means for me is a commitment to this inner path, a commitment to finding what my particular place is, what that actually means, and then a commitment to living that as best I can or as best I understand it. It is recognising that when I do that, I'm living a path that is authentic, that rings true not just for me but for a bigger pattern of things of which I am a small part. But that bigger pattern also needs me to live my part responsibly, and deeply, if it is to unfold to its full design.

Tim Kearney: In concrete terms, does 'finding one's place' encompass work, family, relationship?

Michael Kearney: Yes, it manifests in all those areas. I really like that phrase 'finding one's place'. It reminds me of a wonderful poem by the North American poet, Mary Oliver. It's called 'The Wild Geese'. Here it is:

You do not have to be good.
You do not have to walk on your knees
for a hundred miles through the desert, repenting.
You only have to let the soft animal of your body

love what it loves.
Tell me about despair, yours, and I will tell you mine.
Meanwhile the world goes on.
Meanwhile the sun and the clear pebbles of the rain
are moving across the landscapes,
over the prairies and the deep trees,
the mountains and the rivers.
Meanwhile the wild geese, high in the clean blue air,
are heading home again.
Whoever you are, no matter how lonely,
the world offers itself to your imagination,
calls to you like the wild geese, harsh and exciting –
over and over announcing your place
in the family of things.

It's as though we are born into our human family and those relationships are pivotal and crucial and fundamental. Part of what the inner work and what spirituality means to me is finding one's place in the family of things, finding our place in that deeper matrix of which we are all part – and I love that word 'matrix', because for me it includes the idea of the great mother, the divine mother, that's so present in nature.

It's about finding our place in nature and within nature. With this comes a profound sense of significance, of meaning, of being part of a bigger picture, and a huge respect for otherness, whether that other is a person or a plant or an animal.

So a deep respect for our fellow beings and the planet of which we are part, a sort of deep inner-ecology of spirit, as others have described it.

Tim Kearney: What, in your view, is the core value of Christian spirituality?

Michael Kearney: I think for me the key aspect of Christian spirituality is the connection between suffering and meaning. It seems to me that Christianity is centred around the fundamental truth that the way through to the fullness of life is actually by becoming more profoundly human, by including all of who we are and by recognising that, in a strange and paradoxical way, it's in our fundamental weakness and limits that we can find a way through. For me it's not about glorifying or wallowing in suffering but about recognising that in including these aspects of ourselves we're including the core of our humanity. As we do this, something that is connected to us and that is more than us – and that in the Christian tradition is personalised in Christ and his spirit – may enter the depths of our being and bring us into healing.

*A native of Cork, **Donie Hurley** has been a member of the L'Arche community in Cork since 1985. He works in the Mercy Hospital as a porter on a part-time basis, and he also works part-time in the L'Arche workshop. He plays an active role as a lay pastoral assistant in the L'Arche community in Cork. He is a gifted singer, storyteller and a man of prayer. He currently lives in a house in the L'Arche community.*

THEY WILL HAVE PEACE
LIVING TOGETHER

An Interview with Donie Hurley, 1999

Tim Kearney: Donie, tell me about your story before you came to L'Arche.

Donie Hurley: My father was an accordion player and my mother used to make crochet until she went blind. She often made a wedding dress for people. I was very close to her. She is dead now. I miss her very much and I think about her every day.

Tim Kearney: Why was it that you had to go to Greenmount Industrial School?

Donie Hurley: The mother couldn't keep us, because of her blindness. She fell on the back of her head and they couldn't do anything for her. That caused her blindness.

Tim Kearney: Then you went to Greenmount. Did you have to sleep there? How old were you?

Donie Hurley: I did sleep there and everything. I was about twelve years old. They were very saucy, the Christian Brothers.

Tim Kearney: Were they unhappy years for you?

Donie Hurley: They were. The hardest thing was when you
                    wouldn't be let out. Not being able to visit your
                    family. You wouldn't have any friends to call to
                    see you.
                        I had one friend, Margaret, she was a cousin
                    of mine – she used to bring us out and bring us
                    back again. But I didn't have any friends in the
                    school. It was a very lonely time.

Tim Kearney: Then you went to live with the Lehane family.

Donie Hurley: I had to go to live with the Lehane family,
                    because I had no one to take me and nowhere to
                    go.

Tim Kearney: Did the Lehanes sort of adopt you then?

Donie Hurley: They did. I stayed a long time with them. In the
                    end, I was blamed for taking £15 out of the
                    drawer. I never took it. That's why I had to leave.
                    My cousin Willy worked in the Corporation and
                    his son got me the flat. I was happy there. But
                    when the gambling started I couldn't stay there. I
                    couldn't manage.

Tim Kearney: Why did you want to move out of the flat? Were
                    you lonely?

Donie Hurley: I was, yes, I had no one to come in to visit me.
                    One time the St Vincent de Paul people came but
                    I didn't want them to come in. I didn't have any
                    friends in the flat and that's why I wanted to
                    come to L'Arche.

Tim Kearney: You came to live in L'Arche in 1985. What can you remember about that?

Donie Hurley: Well, I remember you and I remember Mary McCarthy and everybody that was there. I liked the people very much. I can look back on that now today with happiness.

Tim Kearney: What for you, Donie, are the hard things about living in community?

Donie Hurley: The hard things are saying goodbye to people. Saying goodbye to the assistants who have lived with us. And saying goodbye to people that have gone to the other side, like John Cogan, people who have died.

Tim Kearney: What for you are the good things about living in community?

Donie Hurley: The good things are living with other people and helping Fr Joe with the Mass.

Tim Kearney: You have a role in the community as a lay pastoral minister and that means that you assist Fr Joe celebrate the Mass.

Donie Hurley: That's wonderful for me. I like that. I like the priests in Togher too when I am with them to help.

Tim Kearney: You work in the Mercy Hospital in Cork – how many years have you been doing this work?

Donie Hurley: I think it's fifteen years. I'm a porter. I take bloods and urine samples down to the labs, and all the extras and stuff, and back up again when they are wanted. I talk to patients as well. I just ask them how are they, are they having a good day and all this. But I just have to mention Sr Felicitas and the staff – how good they are to me. For instance now this morning – I showed them the note that you gave me about the book that you are writing and they said 'Congratulations Donie, you're in the book'.

Tim Kearney: Do you enjoy your work in the Mercy Hospital?

Donie Hurley: I enjoy it because I have the strength to do it.

Tim Kearney: Donie, what for you is the secret to being happy and contented as a person?

Donie Hurley: Just enjoying yourself and having joy in yourself. When you hear laughter. Laughter is good. It's about having friends. Here in Cork and Dublin and Kilkenny and other places all over the world.

Tim Kearney: What for you, Donie, is the most important thing about being a Christian?

Donie Hurley: Loving Jesus and loving Mary. And loving people. And bear with it.

Tim Kearney: You have been praying for a L'Arche community in Belfast and are very happy that this will be happening soon. Why are you so keen to see one in Belfast?

Donie Hurley: People can go and visit. People can go up and visit and make freedom with them. Make friends with them, like myself, and Danny and Angela and Joe and Valerie and Fr Joe. To visit them and make contact with them. To keep in contact with them.

Tim Kearney:　　Do you think peace will come to Northern Ireland?

Donie Hurley:　　It will. I can see when there is a L'Arche community in Belfast, I can see the peace coming back then. Because the Catholics and the Protestants that we know who will be living in the house will bring peace in themselves – they might have a fight now and again but they will have peace living together.

Tim Kearney:　　Do you think it is possible for Catholics and Protestants to live together in peace?

Donie Hurley:　　I certainly do.

Tim Kearney:　　How would you like to be remembered as a person?

Donie Hurley:　　I'd like to be remembered as the way I am. The way I am today. Just as I am today. I believe in the peace of God and everything.

CHARTER OF THE COMMUNITIES OF L'ARCHE

L'Arche began in 1964 when Jean Vanier and Father Thomas Philippe, in response to a call from God, invited Raphael Simi and Philippe Seux, two men with mental handicaps, to come and share their life in the spirit of the Gospel and of the Beatitudes that Jesus preached.

From this first community, born in France and in the Roman Catholic tradition, many other communities have developed in various cultural and religious traditions.

These communities, called into being by God, are united by the same vision and the same spirit of welcome, of sharing and simplicity.

I Aims

1. The aim of l'Arche is to create communities which welcome people with a mental handicap. By this means l'Arche seeks to respond to the distress of those who are too often rejected, and to give them a valid place in society.

2. L'Arche seeks to reveal the particular gifts of people with a mental handicap, who belong at the very heart of their communities and who call others to share their lives.

3. L'Arche knows that it cannot welcome everyone who has a mental handicap. It seeks to offer not a solution but a sign, a sign that a society, to be truly human, must be founded on welcome and respect for the weak and the downtrodden.

4. In a divided world, l'Arche wants to be a sign of hope. Its communities, founded on covenant relationships between people of differing intellectual capacity, social origin, religion and culture, seek to be a sign of unity, faithfulness and reconciliation.

II Fundamental principles

1.   Whatever their gifts or their limitations, people are all bound together in a common humanity. Everyone is of unique and sacred value, and everyone has the same dignity and the same rights. The fundamental rights of each person include the rights to life, to care, to a home, to education and to work. Also, since the deepest need of a human being is to love and to be loved, each person has a right to friendship, to communion and to a spiritual life.

2.   If human beings are to develop their abilities and talents to the full, realising all their potential as individuals, they need an environment that fosters personal growth. They need to form relationships with others within families and communities. They need to live in an atmosphere of trust, security and mutual affection. They need to be valued, accepted and supported in real and warm relationships.

3.   People with a mental handicap often possess qualities of welcome, wonderment, spontaneity and directness. They are able to touch hearts and to call others to unity through their simplicity and vulnerability. In this way they are a living reminder to the wider world of the essential values of the heart without which knowledge, power and action lose their meaning and purpose.

4.   Weakness and vulnerability in a person, far from being an obstacle to union with God, can foster it. It is often through weakness, recognised and accepted, that the liberating love of God is revealed.

5.   In order to develop the inner freedom to which all people are called, and to grow in union with God, each person needs to have the opportunity of being rooted and nourished in a religious tradition.

III The communities
1. Communities of faith

1.1 L'Arche communities are communities of faith, rooted in prayer and trust in God. They seek to be guided by God and by their weakest members, through whom God's presence is revealed. Each community member is encouraged to discover and deepen his or her spiritual life and live it according to his or her particular faith and tradition. Those who have no religious affiliation are also welcomed and respected in their freedom of conscience.

1.2 Communities are either of one faith or inter-religious. Those that are Christian are either of one Church or inter-denominational. Each community maintains links with the appropriate religious authorities and its members are integrated with local churches or other places of worship.

1.3 Communities recognise that they have an ecumenical vocation and a mission to work for unity.

2. Called to unity

2.1 Unity is founded on the covenant of love to which God calls all the community members. This implies welcome and respect for differences. Such unity presupposes that the person with a handicap is at the centre of community life.

    This unity is built up over time and through faithfulness. Communities commit themselves to accompany their members (once their membership is confirmed) throughout their lives, if this is what those members want.

2.2 Home life is at the heart of a l'Arche community. The different members of a community are called to be one body. They live, work, pray and celebrate together, sharing their joys and their suffering and forgiving each other, as in a family. They have a simple lifestyle which gives priority to relationships.

2.3 The same sense of communion unites the various communities throughout the world. Bound together by solidarity and mutual commitment, they form a worldwide family.

3. Called to growth

3.1 L'Arche communities are places of hope. Each person, according to his or her own vocation, is encouraged to grow in love, self-giving and wholeness, as well as in independence, competence and the ability to make choices.

3.2 The communities wish to secure for their members education, work and therapeutic activities that will be a source of dignity, growth and fulfilment for them.

3.3 The communities wish to provide their members with the means to develop their spiritual life and to deepen their union with and love of God and other people.

3.4 All community members are invited to participate, as far as possible, in decisions concerning them.

4. Integrated in society

4.1 L'Arche communities are open and welcoming to the world around them. They form an integral part of life in their localities, and seek to foster relationships with neighbours and friends.

4.2 The communities seek to be competent in all the tasks they are called to accomplish.

4.3 The communities wish to enable people with a handicap to work, believing work to be an important means of integration.

4.4 The communities seek to work closely with:
- the families and guardians of people who are handicapped,
- professionals,
- government authorities,

and with all those who work in a spirit of justice and peace for people who are handicapped.

IV Conclusion

L'Arche is deeply concerned by the distress of people who suffer injustice and rejection because they are handicapped. This concern should impel the communities of l'Arche to do all they can to defend the rights of people with a mental handicap, to support the creation of places of welcome for them, and to call on our society to become more just and respectful towards them. The communities of l'Arche want to be in solidarity with the poor of the world, and with all those who take part in the struggle for justice.